Praise for

The Pet I Can't Forget

In this beautiful book, Karen A. Anderson and her animal spirit friends provide peace, comfort, and compassionate assistance in the wake of pet loss. Whether you are grieving a companion animal who has died recently, or you feel a connection with one long passed, Anderson reminds us that our pets never truly leave us, the love we feel for them and what they feel for us are eternal, and we can experience their ongoing presence in our lives when we know what to look for. If you've lost a beloved companion animal, this book can help you shift your story from one of sorrow to one of peace and a love that never dies.

Karen Frazier
Author & Intuitive Energy Healer

Karen A. Anderson's book explores the eternal connection we share with our beloved animal companions with awe-inspiring stories that will open your heart to healing and open your mind to discovering more signs from the afterlife.

Sandra Champlain

Author of the #1 International Bestseller, "We Don't Die - A Skeptic's Discovery of Life After Death," host of "We Don't Die Radio" and "Shades of the Afterlife."

Having to physically say goodbye to a beloved animal is one of life's enduring hardships. As an animal lover, I have experienced this many times, most recently with the transition of my beautiful cat, Kayli. Physical death cannot interfere with the eternal bonds we have with our cherished pets. While their bodies may be gone, their vibrant souls live on within our hearts and precious memories.

Karen A. Anderson is a celebrated author and animal communicator. In her new book, The Pet I Can't Forget, she expertly guides her readers to acknowledge and understand how animals communicate with us from the afterlife and beyond. Karen is well qualified to write a book of this magnitude as she understands this genre deeply.

She takes your hand and speaks to your heart as she familiarizes you with the various signs from the afterlife and how they can provide hope and healing.

The Pet I Can't Forget is a gripping masterpiece showcasing the magnificent ways our animals connect with us in spirit. Savor the pages within and let the healing magic happen.

Nicole Strickland

Afterlife & Paranormal Researcher | Bestselling Author | Award-Winning Podcaster | Public Speaker

The Pet
I Can't Forget

Finding Hope and Healing

With Signs From the Afterlife

Karen A. Anderson

The Amazing Afterlife of Animals

Also available in German translation:

"Tierbotschaften aus dem Jenseits

Verbluffende Beweise und Zeichen"

Also Available in Korean Translation

Chinese Translation Available in 2024

The author of this book does not dispense medical or psychiatric advice and only offers information of a general nature to procure healing and closure after a loss. This book is not designed to be a definitive guide or substitute for qualified professionals, and there is no guarantee that the methods suggested in this book will be successful, as healing is a personal journey. The author and publisher do not assume liability for any outcomes that may be sustained by the methods described in this book, and any such liability is hereby expressly disclaimed. In the event you use any of the information in this book for yourself, the author and the publisher assume no responsibility for your actions.

Interior Layout: Beloved Publishing House

Cover Design: Rose Miller

Printed in the United States of America

First Printing: 2023

ISBN: 9798862507737

Publisher: Painted Rain Publishing

Dedication

To all who have loved and lost a beloved companion and
believe that true love never dies.

To my precious departed companion angels

for their guidance and insight.

Foreword

By Katie Lawlor, Psy.D.

My rabbit Gem changed the course of my life.

I remember the first time I saw him. It was the summer of 2016; I was in graduate school training to become a clinical psychologist and had been studying at a neighborhood coffee shop. As I walked home that sunny afternoon, I decided to pass by the animal shelter, and there he was – crouched in a small cage near the front window.

I walked in and literally gasped out loud – he was the most beautiful creature I had ever seen. He was a tiny white Netherland Dwarf Rabbit with soft pink ears and sparkling blue eyes.

The volunteer working explained to me that a mother with three young boys had surrendered him earlier that day; she was concerned they were not yet old enough to be responsible for him. "Is he looking for a home?" I asked, still in awe of being so close to perfection. "Oh yes," the volunteer responded, "we are hoping to find him one by the close of today." In that very moment, we became a family, with Gem joining his big brother Bear (a scruffy 10-pound terrier-mix adopted from the Sacramento SPCA in 2011).

We would share four beautiful years together (Gem was five when he adopted me), and he was by my side during a heartrending, adrift time in my life – the end of a long-term relationship, a parent diagnosed with cancer, the self-doubt and debt of academia. I came to count on his pure and unconditional love, how he'd snuggle up for a pet when I sat on the carpet to read, or how he'd thump in the middle of the night if it got too dark in our rented room near campus in Palo Alto.

Gem died unexpectedly on the morning of Saturday, August 29, 2020. What strikes me about that day is how your entire world can go dark while you're drinking your coffee.

That first night, I kept waking up, expecting to find him gently sleeping at the foot of my bed. When he wasn't there, I sank into depths of loneliness that scared me.

After wandering aimlessly through life and all of its commitments the next few weeks, I decided to get away for the weekend; I drove to the remote Northern California coastal town of Bodega Bay, known for its grey fog and lashing waves. I needed to be in a place that felt as raw and cold as I was. Sitting on the porch of the little cabin, I asked Gem to send me an unmistakable sign to assure me he was safe and free. The latter was especially important because I had learned from his veterinarian that he was most likely blind when he passed.

A few moments later, a jackrabbit sprinted across the open field that stretched down to the sea; He first stopped to gaze at me, and then turned his head toward the water, almost as if he, too, was watching the sunset. He lingered a few more seconds before darting through a patch of wildflowers and then into the forest beyond. In that moment, I knew my boy had come to visit, and would anytime I asked him to be near.

If you are experiencing grief – months or even years -- following the loss of your beloved companion animal, please know it's because you are still experiencing love.

This love does not fade with time, and this book shows us how we can embrace this enduring connection.

While they were alive, our animals loved us wholeheartedly and with such joy. While they are no longer physically with us they would want us to live meaningful and fulfilling lives, as we did when they were by our sides.

Finally, in addition to bringing comfort and peace, this book reminds us to ask ourselves what our animals would want for us, and how they would want us to feel. In this way, we can cherish their spirit until we are reunited with them once more. This time, forever.

Katie Lawlor, Psy.D.

Shanti Project Veterinary Mental Health Initiative

Instagram - @petlosspsychologist

Beyond Grateful!

Acknowledgements

I am eternally grateful to everyone who shared their stories for this book. Each interview was recorded via Zoom to capture the details and depths of emotions.

Most of these experiences had never been shared with me, and hearing about them for the first time brought tears, laughter, and so much insight into how healing afterlife messages can be.

The courage and willingness to revisit some of their most painful moments so that others may find inspiration is a true testament to their generosity. Please forgive me for any omissions or oversights. They were not intentional. I am humbled and honored to share your stories.

Listed in no particular order with permission.

Special thanks to Frank Grine, Beth Reinstein, Danielle Turtainen, Antonette Perry, Dedria Brashear, Linda N., Anne Farnbacher, Judy Philip, Teresa Steward, Jayne Welsh, Jeremy Cavanaugh, Vicki Imperati, Nicole Santostefano, Melissa Murray, Brandon Morrison, Brenda Dickmann, Keith Owens, Sandra Reed, Kenya Lopez, Cassandra Vazquez, Cindee Von-Lehe Thomas, Kerry Robinson, Debbie Rendek, Jo Jordan, Carolyn Rossi, Russell Moffatt, Bethany Ullig, Jarka Brinkman, Artemis Davitian-Derk, Cassie Michele Baker, Liza Nyhuis, Karen Estabrook, Donna Marie Serianni, Carolena Hollifield, Patricia Goss, Ellie Hansen, Victoria Dahl, Joan Rourke, Karen Howenstein, Rhian Clark, Carrie Purcell Smith, Karen DeSimone, Kristina Bergvall, Ann Christine.

A special thanks to Katie Lawlor, Psy.D. for writing the beautiful foreword. Katie's vast knowledge and expertise in the psychology of grief and loss embody the journey we embark upon when we say goodbye to a beloved companion.

Contents

Introduction

I am unfixable.

I go into seclusion and hide from the world when I grieve. When one of my beloved companions takes their last breath, I do not want to be around anyone.

I seek refuge with my other animals.

I rarely share the depths of emotions that I feel or post all about it on social media.

I would rather hone my skills at being a hermit and find peace in solitary seclusion on my mountaintop.

Grief is not fixable.

I am not broken in that sense.

In the emotional, heartache sense, yes, I am totally shattered.

While condolences are appreciated, I do not want to hear about the bright side and all I should be grateful for.

Attempts to cheer me up are futile.

Just let me be in pain.

Acknowledge where I am and what I am feeling.

That is what I need.

Join me where I am at by saying:

"I'm sorry this is happening to you. Do you want to talk about it?"

Even though the answer will probably be no, let me hurt.

I feel better when you give me that space just to be.

It goes against what we usually do, right?

I know. I'm guilty.

I have tried to fix others who reached out to me when their world came to a halt.

There are no fixes when it comes to matters of the heart.

Sometimes just being a soft place to fall is all that is needed.

Let those around you know what you need in challenging times.

They likely have *no clue* how to help you, but they *want* to help you.

If you don't know what you need, tell them that too.

It is okay not to be okay.

This is my acknowledgement to you and all the unfixable souls.

I am so sorry for your loss. You must be devastated. I am so sorry you are in so much pain. I am here for you.

I have written this book for those who believe love transcends physical death. For those who have even a glimmer of hope, departed loved ones communicate with us in amazing and creative ways.

And finally, for those who are ready, willing, and open to receive signs from the afterlife.

This is not a book about grief or how to cope with those feelings. I will leave that to the experts.

This book is about signs from the afterlife, how incredibly healing they are, and how you can receive more signs from your companions.

Throughout the chapters, you will discover that signs are everywhere, and by simply acknowledging them, you open the door to receiving more.

Even if you don't think you have received any signs, there will also be insight for you.

When I started writing this book, my goal was to help others who are incapacitated after a loss. By sharing actual afterlife signs from the animals' perspective, I hope an entire new world will unfold for you.

While I was writing the manuscript, I tried to think of a title that would honor departed companions and represent the dignity they deserved.

Most often, companion animals are referred to as our pets. However, I am not a fan of the word *pet*, as our companions are so much more than that. Upon further research, it became clear with algorithms, search engines, and titles that had already been published, the choices were limited and ultimately, I decided on the word *pet* in the title.

I also do not favor the word *owner* and refer to you as their mom or dad. Our companions are family and for those of us who do not have human children, they are the closest bonds we have to that human-child connection throughout our lives.

My greatest wish is for you to find the hope and healing you deserve in the following chapters.

We may love them all, but one pet, our soulmate, rises above all others.

Of course, we will never forget any of them, as they are all so precious.

But there will always be that pet we can't forget.

A note to the reader:

When you turn the page, the narration will shift to the perspective of the beloved animal companion in your life. In the final chapters, I will narrate once more and share actual afterlife sessions conducted over the past twenty-six years.

Chapter 1

Gone

And just like that, I was gone.

Nothing could prepare you for the moment I took my last breath or the emptiness that followed.

Let me put your mind at ease right away. You do not have to worry about me. I am safe and perfect in every way, surrounded by my beautiful afterlife.

You were my happiest hello and my hardest goodbye.

Your world may have shattered the day I died, but a powerful bond activated when I left. A bond so strong that time or distance cannot keep us apart.

Our souls connected long before we met and will stay together long after this story ends.

Something magical happened somewhere in between — something so unique and unlike anything else you have ever experienced.

There may be other beloved companions who stole your heart, but I am the pet you can't forget. I hold the key to your heart and soul.

As the caretaker of this sacred key, my mission is to always be there for you in life and the afterlife. I will never leave you.

This may feel like the end of our story or seem like I am gone forever, but you are about to discover it is just the beginning, and we can continue our journey until we are together again someday.

Chapter 2

Only Love Matters

love

Losing me may be *the most devastating loss* you have ever endured. Whatever led up to my final moments, things likely beyond our control do not matter.

I never think about those things, and I wish you didn't either.

There is only one thing that matters — our love.

Our beautiful connection matters more than anything else. We had an incredible experience that no one understood except us.

I will share everything I can to help you overcome the heaviness and lingering pain. I wish I could take it all away, but no one has the power to do that.

Your inner turmoil may linger for days, weeks, months, or longer, but those sharp edges will soften when you know I am near.

I have also called upon a trusted friend, Karen Anderson, to join us on this journey. Karen has helped thousands of bereaved pet parents find peace after a loss.

Although neither of us are grief experts, Karen and I have the same goal: *To show you how to become aware of my presence and receive more signs*.

Karen has gathered awe-inspiring stories from pet parents who have also endured a loss.

The evidential messages and the signs they received from their unforgettable companions will allow you to find a way through the darkness.

Some stories will make you laugh, and others will probably make you cry.

Their experiences may differ from ours, but hidden messages buried within these chapters are designed to light the path ahead to restore balance in your life.

In the end, we separate only in physical form.

Matters of the heart and soul are not a one-size-fits-all affair. It may take a while before anything brings you comfort.

Please don't give up because I will never give up on you.

You will never be the same because a loss changes everything. It will be different now, but what happens next is just the continuation of our story.

Everyone has a unique experience while healing, but hopefully, your worries will drift away once you discover what really happened when I transitioned away from my body.

To sum it all up in a few words, it was magical.

Chapter 3

The Afterlife

It was pure exhilaration when I left my body. The only physical sensation was a slight pressure change. Like when your ears pop on an airplane.

There was no pain, discomfort, or fear.

I was transported into a new weightless dimension upon the last beat of my heart.

I felt more alive than ever as my soul expanded.

A range of emotions enveloped me, from the purest love to complete and utter serenity. It was incredibly soothing, like being immersed in a warm bubble bath.

I was immediately greeted by loved ones, both human and animal. There were also a few other beings of light that welcomed me. I felt their love and kindness as I whisked around in delight.

The afterlife is a parallel dimension slightly above your ground level. Time and gravity do not exist.

It is lighter, softer, and endless. This dimension overlaps your world, so when things line up just right, you can capture a glimpse of me from the corner of your eye.

I vanish just as fast when our worlds move out of alignment.

Just because you cannot see me does not mean I am gone.

Scientists have an explanation for this, which has something to do with the light spectrum or quantum physics. Those topics are way out of my league, so I will stick to my area of expertise.

Your energy looks like millions of twinkling stars.

I can still see you because a brilliant glow radiates from your heart center. Your light is visible to me no matter where I am in the Universe or beyond.

The colors around you change with your emotions. You sparkle the most when you are smiling and happy.

If you want to see me more clearly, soften your gaze.

Shift your focus slightly above or to the side where your eyes are drawn. This allows your mind's eye to see me.

Animals and children are much more adept at seeing spirit energy. They can easily pick up on my presence as I glide between your dimension and mine.

Their ability to sense the slightest change in atmosphere is far more advanced than yours. They may stare at the ceiling or in the corner of a room.

Spirit energy tends to gather in corners just like dust bunnies.

I can hear your voice.

I love it when you say my name and particularly, my nickname. Your voice is irresistible and draws me close to you.

I also understand your thoughts. I use *telepathy* in place of my ears. Telepathy is one of the most common ways I will communicate with you.

Known as mind-to-mind communication, everyone transmits telepathic messages throughout the day, most commonly during their dreams.

When you suddenly think about me

I am letting you know I am near.

There will be moments when you cannot stop thinking about me. While some thoughts are yours, many times, those are messages from me.

I may flash an image into your mind which feels like your own thought. It might be an adventure we shared, a memory, or a single word.

I will always send positive images infused with love.

You may wonder how to tell if it is me or your imagination. Next time ask yourself this question:

Was I thinking about that memory now?

If the answer is no, then that was a message from me.

It is that simple.

We share the same energetic space, and you may not realize I am near.

If you feel a sudden wave of emotions wash over you out of the blue, that is from me too. Your soul recognizes me and responds with a surge of uncontrollable feelings.

These feelings come and go at some of the strangest moments but are always loving.

I am with you on your darkest days.

When you are in pain, I never leave your side. I wait patiently as you move through all the emotions of grief.

You never have to worry about me being alone in the afterlife. Even strays or abandoned animals who do not have a family are met by a loving guide.

Remember, time does not exist in the afterlife. No clocks or calendars define this dimension. I may send you a message when you least expect it.

But what if you don't feel anything?

Does that mean I am not with you?

No, of course not.

It usually means you are still under the numbing grip of grief. It may take a while before you are open to receiving messages or signs from me.

There are three powerful forces that have probably hijacked your thoughts and blocked my messages.

You call them blame, forgiveness, and guilt.

These words are not in my vocabulary, but I will do my best to explain why they are so unnecessary and help you move through them.

Chapter 4

Blame, Forgiveness, and Guilt

I do not blame you for what happened or how my life ended.

You do not need to ask for my forgiveness for your decisions.

There is no need to feel guilty about anything you did or did not do.

Blame, forgiveness, and guilt are human concepts.

It is common to feel some or all of them after losing me. Although these are overwhelming thoughts to you, they do not concern me.

No matter what happened, I could never be upset with you. I love you wholeheartedly, and nothing will ever change that. You did your best. You took care of me and loved me, and nothing surpasses that.

My love for you will never change.

While it is natural to want to be upset about how my life ended, sometimes tragic situations happen. You would never harm me. I know that for a fact. So, please, starting right now, let go of those thoughts.

As they come into your mind, imagine they drift away like a balloon disappearing into the sky.

When you release those negative thoughts, that is when the balance shifts as you are about to discover in this next story.

Chapter 5

Lexi

Carrie sensed something was wrong when she came home after running errands. Her 13-year-old tri-colored border collie, Lexi, did not greet her at the door. Carrie called her name, but there was only a deafening silence. She darted into every room, but she couldn't find Lexi. Panic set in.

Lexi always stayed home alone when Carrie ran errands. The terrible reality of what happened to Lexi sunk in as

Carrie rounded the corner of the laundry room. She tried to wrap her head around what she was seeing. Lexi's lifeless body was on the floor.

Carrie ran to her side and saw something over Lexi's head. A large plastic bag covered her entire face. She ripped the bag off, but it was too late. Lexi was gone.

The feeling of dread washed over her. It was a plastic liner from a box of cereal. Carrie left the box on the floor next to the garbage can in the kitchen for the recycle bin. Lexi had never gotten into the recycling boxes before. She must have tried reaching the crumbs inside when the plastic liner got stuck over her face.

The pain from this tragic loss was so intense Carrie could barely breathe. She cried for days, and she blamed herself relentlessly. Horrible thoughts looped through her mind.

She had left empty cereal boxes on the floor many times before, and Lexi never touched them.

As time went by Carrie's pain turned into anger. She was mad at herself, and guilt consumed her. She felt responsible for Lexi's death.

About a week later, Carrie was compelled to go outside to be close to Lexi. She looked up at the sky and saw a lone cloud above her. To her amazement, the cloud began to morph into the shape of Lexi's face.

A soft pink glow surrounded the cloud, and Carrie sensed her angel was nearby. She wondered what happens to animals when they die. She never thought about the afterlife and, until now, did not believe such a place existed.

After seeing that cloud, Carrie was compelled to search for answers about the afterlife. She needed something to help her move forward. As if guided by Lexi, she found Karen's Animal Communication practice group on Facebook. That decision would be a pivotal moment that changed her life forever.

In the group, photos of pets are posted so members can practice their communication skills. Carrie quickly learned the simple steps of connecting with the animals and was surprised when she received accurate messages. As this new world unfolded, the pain began to lift.

Carrie's world turned upside down when another group member, Rhian, communicated with Lexi. During their session, Lexi shared the image of a beautiful peacock. The odd message didn't make sense, but Carrie kept an open mind and filed that away in her mind. Rhian also encouraged Carrie to work with an energy healer to help her process her grief.

Intrigued, Carrie found one of the only energy healers in her area and booked an appointment. Weeks later, Carrie drove to the studio and was welcomed by a friendly female staff member. As they walked through the lobby, the woman turned to Carrie with a smile and said, *"Look at this beautiful window."*

Carrie stared in disbelief at the stained-glass window. It was decorated with a colorful peacock design. Dumbfounded and amazed, Carrie remembered the strange message of a peacock from Lexi. Riddled with goosebumps and a surge of emotions, Carrie knew it was a sign from Lexi.

It was suddenly clear that she needed to let go of blaming herself to finally move forward on her healing journey. The synchronicity was unbelievable.

Carrie's heart opened when she realized Lexi was still with her and that spurred more afterlife signs.

It was a cold winter day, and the trees were covered in a thick blanket of snow. Carrie was seeking solitude at a park near her home and aching with sadness thinking about Lexi.

"Okay, Lex," Carrie said, "If you're here and with me now, show me a *red cardinal*."

A few minutes later, a red cardinal landed in a nearby tree. Carrie could not believe her eyes. She was overcome with joy as tears streamed down her face. She sensed Lexi's energy all around her like a warm hug.

One day, Carrie was driving along and once again felt Lexi's spirit. A wave of love washed over her, and she heard a clear message in her mind.

"You need to have more fun."

Carrie smiled because she tends to be too serious, so she took this message to heart. The next song on the radio was *Dancing Queen, by Abba.* Carrie cranked up the volume and sang along as loud as she could, ditty-bopping down the road.

Carrie's life has changed in dramatic ways since Lexi's tragic accident. She has found confidence in herself and now prioritizes her goals and dreams. It has taken some time to heal, but Carrie let go of the blame.

That one decision to take action to discover more about animal communication changed the course of her journey. Lexi was so much more than what happened to her. She was intelligent, funny, and such a sweet girl and Carrie refused to let Lexi's beautiful life be overshadowed by how she died. Lexi deserved to be honored for who she was.

Carrie welcomed two new dogs, Harry, and Gretchen, into the family. The sweet sound of paws on the floor has once again filled her home.

Chapter 6

How Signs Are Sent

There are many creative ways I send signs and messages from the afterlife. While some signs are so subtle you barely notice them, others are so obvious you cannot deny them. Most will fall somewhere in the middle.

I can do amazing things in the afterlife.

There are no restrictive barriers as there are on Earth. I can go everywhere you go. I can ride next to you in the car and listen as you sing along to the radio. I can go to work with you or watch what you buy at the grocery store. I follow you on your walks and snuggle into bed when you do. I don't miss a thing because now I can experience everything with you.

It is easier to send signs when your energy is balanced.

To send a sign I need a source of energy. Most of the time, that source is you. I can search for other fuel sources, such as electronic equipment, but I prefer your energy. You are familiar to me, and your energy reminds me of home.

When your energy is low, mine will be too. Sometimes I must wait until your pain subsides before I send a sign.

Do not be discouraged if you have not received any signs.

It is not a lack of love or the end of our story. There is far more to it than that. Not every departed companion sends signs or messages, especially those that spend the most time with you.

It is so important to acknowledge the tiniest sign you receive. That fills my spiritual fuel tank allowing me to send more signs.

Think about the gas tank in your car. With a full tank, you can go anywhere and travel a long way. But when your tank is empty, you won't get very far.

To help me store fuel reserves, surround yourself with anything that comforts your heart. It does not have to be fancy, like gardening, walking, or listening to soothing music.

Living signs appear when I am still alive.

Signs can appear at any time, including while I am still alive. A living sign is as powerful as an afterlife sign and can help you through a difficult time. You may see a rainbow or a cloud formation. You may have a sudden unexplained sense of knowing that provides clarity and insight. Think of living signs as ways to let you know you are doing the right thing or making the right choice.

Living signs are obvious with powerful messages and are filled with an incredible amount of love.

Connect the Dots

When you connect the dots to every dream, sensation, or unexplainable event it becomes clear something unique is happening around you. The collection of all those moments, especially the goosebumps moments, removes any doubt that I am near.

When signs are disregarded, or you think it is your imagination I lose momentum. It takes time to refuel my spiritual tank. But I am persistent, and I will keep trying.

Coincidence

I believe there is no such thing as coincidence. I am always looking for ways to connect with you, so it is important to trust what you receive. The more closely you pay attention, the more you will see, sense, or hear. Trust is the crucial component of staying connected with me. Keep a positive outlook and state that you are ready to believe and excited to receive a sign.

Once enough energy has been gathered and the timing is right, I will send you a sign. Before we get to all the signs I can send, this is how you can tell it was from me.

Who sent the sign?

All your departed loved ones, family or friends, humans, and animals, are part of your soul group. All of us can send signs. So how do you know who sent it?

What resonates the most at that moment.

Multiple loved ones may send messages, especially when you are grieving. So, pay attention to your first impressions. What resonated with you the moment you received that sign will likely indicate who sent it.

We each have a unique sign, like a calling card infused with our specific energy fingerprint.

To determine who sent a particular sign, ask for clarity. Such as, "If that was you, kitty, make the lights flicker again." If nothing happens, then it may be from someone else. Rephrase the question to someone else, such as, "If that was you, Mom, do it again."

When you ask for clarity, be loving, positive, and patient. It just may be that you received a big message of love from everyone in your soul group. Lucky you!

We do not get discouraged if you mistakenly think someone else sent you a sign. Your soul group rejoices that you acknowledged the message, which fuels all of us and sends out a massive loving wave of energy.

Watch for repeating signs to appear.

Repeating patterns are as essential in life as they are in the afterlife, and I love to send repetitive signs. I may only send you ladybugs while someone else in your soul group sends rainbows. We all have our favorites. When you receive a repeating sign that usually indicates a specific calling card.

Interpreting a Sign

An afterlife sign speaks volumes in its purest form. A feeling or sense of knowing usually accompanies them. Pay close attention to your initial impression. It is usually the most accurate. If you receive a message, you do not understand, ask for clarity.

Sometimes I can share more details or provide additional insight. You can also write a note asking for clarity and place it beside your bed. The answers you seek may appear in your dreams or be fresh on your mind when you wake up.

Afterlife signs lose their purity when you attempt to interpret them or put a logical spin on them. Trust your first impressions for the best results and avoid overthinking.

Now, let's talk about all the different types of signs I send. There are so many different signs, more than I can cover in this book, but I will share the most common ones and a few of my favorites.

Chapter 7

Animals, Birds, and Butterflies

Animal signs include all types of wildlife, reptiles, insects, and birds. When I send an animal sign, our souls connect instantly. There will be no doubt in your mind that something unique is happening.

There will be a significant surge of emotions when you see them, and your soul will react to my presence. You may feel goosebumps or instantly think about me. Those are some of my favorite moments.

Animals

I may send unique animals like turtles, lizards, or squirrels. I always look for the perfect opportunity to send a sign wherever you go. The animals enjoy the experience and are honored to be part of our journey. Sometimes I have permission to share their body to deliver a message and other times I hop on for a brief ride and let you know I am near.

Birds

Birds fall into the animal category but have another layer of intrigue. Birds are known throughout many cultures to be spirit messengers. They serve as a link between the earthly realm and the spirit realm. Their ability to fly associates them with heaven, winged angels, spirit guides, and God.

You may see a robin, cardinal, hummingbird, or hawk. It may be a singular encounter or a series of them. Birds may appear unconcerned with your presence. That fearlessness is intentional to grab your attention.

Butterflies, Dragonflies, and Ladybugs

Butterflies may flutter near you or even land on you. I also send dragonflies, ladybugs, and other insects as signs. Dragonflies may land on or near you or hover in an orchestrated dance. You may see one or a hundred all at once.

Ladybugs are spirit messengers bringing good luck your way. Seeing ladybugs often, in odd places, or during the colder months when they are generally dormant is an obvious sign I am near.

In this next story, a dog named Bill Bayley sends a multitude of signs to announce his presence, from butterflies to his name.

Chapter 8

Bill Bayley

Bill watched the birds fly into the distance as the sun set over the lake. It would be his last trip to their favorite cabin in Bavaria. Jayne and her partner Anne would say goodbye to their beloved fourteen-year-old black Labrador retriever in just a few days. Bill's health was deteriorating rapidly, and they wanted to savor every moment together.

Every summer, they vacationed at the lake. It was a magical place that held a lifetime of memories. They sat quietly in those last bittersweet moments as they watched the orange glow fade into the night sky.

Jayne met Bill at a breeding facility in the United Kingdom when he was a puppy. She was looking for the right dog to be a part of her program for school-aged children. Bill was friendly, intelligent, and gentle with children. He was perfect in every way. After graduating from therapy dog training, he grew into a loving, athletic dog.

Bill was wise beyond his years and understood complete sentences. He had no desire to bolt off into the fields when he was off leash and preferred the company of his family. Bill loved to sleep in late and he also developed a fondness for sticks.

Bill had a zest for life and beamed with pure happiness, whether it was canoeing, paddleboarding, or hiking. He welcomed every new challenge with an open heart. When Bill was about eleven, Jayne noticed his back paws dragging on the floor as if he could not lift them properly. After extensive testing, a neurological issue was discovered that impacted the nerves along the spine.

Due to his age, surgery was not an option. The recovery would be lengthy, and it was questionable if surgery would resolve the problem. It was devastating news. Bill gradually lost his balance and, ultimately, the use of his hind legs. None of that seemed to matter to Bill. He was happy and healthy in every other way.

Jayne and Anne became full-time caretakers tending to his every need. They got Bill a buggy so he could go on walks with them. He loved it and enjoyed going out in his customized chariot, as they called it. Bill took every setback in stride, and not once did he lose any of that zest or his fondness for sticks.

When the day came to say their final goodbyes, Jayne and Anne gathered in the garden at the cabin and waited for the veterinarian. In their last moments together, Jayne found the strength she never knew she had. It must have come from Bill. He was so stoic and serene. Everyone was calm until the final injection was administered. Without warning, Bill yelped in pain as the serum entered his bloodstream. Jolted by his response, Jayne did her best to comfort him, and within moments, Bill took his last breath.

That night, overwhelmed with pain, Jayne went outside at dusk to clear her mind. The moon was full and bright. She looked to the sky at just the right moment to see a falling star next to the moon. It was a spectacular sight, and she instantly knew Bill was letting her know he arrived at his destination. It was the first of many signs Bill would send.

Jayne searched online for books about the afterlife and started a journal to help her process her emotions. She could not stop thinking about the moment Bill yelped in pain. While she was writing, a single white feather drifted down and landed on her arm. Bill was just getting started with making his presence known.

Reading about the afterlife helped Jayne understand what happens at the end of life. She discovered that the pain from the injection would not be part of Bill's memory. That created a tremendous positive shift. Letting go of that terrible moment freed her from the prison of grief.

The feather signs continued to appear in the strangest ways. A car next to her at the lake had dozens of white feathers scattered all over the dashboard. When she brought Bill's cremated remains home, she was met by a sea of white feathers around the driveway, the roof, and the garden. There was no logical explanation for so many feathers scattered around. White feathers have also appeared on the pathways where they walked with Bill.

The synchronicities continued as Bill's name appeared in unusual places. Butterflies appeared frequently and fluttered playfully around them. They also saw butterflies in decor on the walls, in photos, on signs, and as artwork wherever they went.

Jayne and Anne were at a restaurant with a friend, talking about the signs Bill had sent when Anne noticed the painting on the wall above them. The name BILL was in the left corner, and the number five appeared twice in gold lettering. Bill's birthday was January 5th, 2005.

After all these signs, Jayne realized that she would never lose Bill. That bond cannot be broken. He lives on in her heart and soul. By honoring his memory and how stoically Bill faced all his debilitating issues, Jayne has found the once elusive peace. Bill lived each day with zest and happiness, and Jayne consciously decided to live her life the same way.

Chapter 9

Sky Signs

When you sense something magical is happening in the sky, your soul tells you to look up. When grief weighs heavily upon you, I may send a big sign in the sky.

Sky signs, like rainbows and shooting stars, reflect how connected you and I are to things beyond our physical bodies. We are part of something much grander and vast. We are limitless spiritual beings with access to multiple dimensions. Everything you and I experienced was purposeful or precious in some way. We were destined to be together in this lifetime.

Sky signs connect directly to your soul at the highest level. Imagine the power of thunderstorms, gravity, or the sun. You are part of that vastness and are stronger than you could possibly imagine.

One of the reasons I am with you in this lifetime is to show you how powerful you are. You are capable of anything you set your mind to.

When you are feeling lost or lonely, look up. Sky signs are all around you.

In the following story, a little white dog sends a big sky sign before he takes his last breath.

Chapter 10

Paddie

"Is it raining?" the male voice asked.

Rhian looked around the kitchen, but no one was there. Her husband, Andrew, was in the garage, so she went looking for him.

"Did you just come inside and ask me if it was raining?" Rhian asked.

"No. Why would I do that?" Andrew asked, "It's boiling hot outside."

Rhian went down the hall and asked her daughters if they had said anything about the rain. The answer was no. Maybe she was hearing things. The waves of grief had consumed her since Paddie died.

Rhian wondered if the male voice could have been Paddie.

Every time they went for a walk, she asked him if it was raining outside because Paddie did not like to walk in the rain.

A sense of wonder came over her. Rhian was familiar with communicating with angels and angel healing, so she was intrigued to find out if animals could also communicate.

She ordered a deck of spirit cards to determine if Paddie was contacting her. When the cards arrived, she anxiously shuffled the deck and pulled her first card. She stared at it in disbelief.

The message on the card said: *I am now your guide.*

Rhian was thrilled. This felt like a message from Paddie. She desperately wanted to know he was okay. Losing him was dreadful and completely changed her.

He wasn't acting like himself. His health had been failing, and he developed arthritis and neurological issues. Rhian knew he was ready to go when he stopped sleeping in his usual spot at the top of the stairs. Even with his declining health, it did not make the decision any easier.

Paddie was a white West Highland terrier, also known as a Westie. When he was a pup, he was adorable but quite a handful. He destroyed their floors, grabbed mouthfuls of her daughter's hair, and howled all night. He loved going for walks except in the rain.

As the years passed, Paddie became the perfect gentleman fiercely loyal to his family. Rhian promised Paddie long ago that she would not keep him here longer than what was comfortable for him. Even though she knew it was the best decision for Paddie, her heart broke into a million pieces on his last day. As the car approached the clinic, a giant cloud hovered directly above them.

Rhian couldn't help but notice it, as the sky seemed to be calling to her. She and Andrew watched in amazement as the cloud formed in the exact shape of Paddie. The resemblance was undeniable.

The doctor came into the room, and they whispered their final goodbyes. Surrounded by his family, Paddie took his last breath.

When they left the clinic to go home, Rhian was shocked to see the same cloud above her. The exact outline of Paddie was visible.

The turmoil that followed sent Rhian into a tailspin. She realized she had struggled with anticipatory grief while Paddie was still alive. Anticipatory grief is sadness, pain, and sorrow when you know the end is near. You anticipate the day of departure and grieve as deeply as when it occurs.

The day she heard the voice everything shifted. Signs began to appear such as the random image of two dogs that popped into her mind. Although she did not recognize either of the dogs at the time, months later, after adopting two new pups, Daisey and Poppie, Rhian realized it was their faces she had seen.

Paddie's messages prompted Rhian to seek more answers beyond her comfort zone. Her thirst for knowledge about the afterlife led her to join Karen's practice group. Learning the simple steps, Rhian embraced her animal communication abilities. In a short time, she was conducting sessions for other members.

Paddie continued to make his presence known in creative ways. His photos magically appear on Rhian's devices, he visits in her dreams, and his image appears in reflections on eyeglasses.

From the first cloud she saw on his last day, Rhian finds comfort in knowing she will always have her trusted guide, Paddie, by her side. Unless, of course, it is raining outside.

Chapter 11

Lily

When Teresa and her husband arrived at the veterinary clinic, they were overwhelmed by what they were about to do. It was time to say goodbye to their beloved black and white cat, Lily.

A bright rainbow appeared above them as they agonized over their impossible decision. The beautiful rainbow was such an unexpected sight. Like a beacon of hope, it was a much-needed sign that this was the right decision. With tears in their eyes, they held Lily close as she took her last breath.

They drove home with an empty cat carrier, burdened by their thoughts. Lily was gone forever. Teresa wandered through the house, unable to do anything. She glanced out the window out of habit, expecting to see Lily in the garden, but no one was there. Her blanket was still on the sofa where she had spent her last night. The house was quiet and so empty.

With the heaviness of grief upon her, Teresa began to question the existence of the afterlife and found several books on the topic. The uplifting stories were comforting and inspired her to learn more.

There had to be more to their connection than the physical bond. The intense pain went on for weeks and made everyday tasks nearly impossible. A significant weight was lifted when Teresa discovered they could still communicate. Lily was not gone forever. Her energy lives on in the afterlife.

Teresa decided to embrace this new perspective and began talking to Lily. She told Lily about her day as if she were beside her. When she went to sleep, she visualized each of her beloved cats and surrounded them with loving thoughts. Once Teresa realized they all continued to thrive on their spiritual journey, Lily made her presence known.

Teresa began to have vivid dreams where she felt Lily's fur. Her dreams were incredibly realistic and so loving. Teresa expected to open her eyes and see Lily in her usual spot.

In a short time, Teresa finally captured a brief glimpse of Lily moving through the house. She saw Lily's sleek black fur with her unmistakable white paws and white around her neck. It was exhilarating to know she was still there.

One day, Teresa's son was in the kitchen making a sandwich when he heard Lily's distinctive vocalization. He turned around, expecting to see her, but no one was there. They knew it was Lily. She loved eating sandwiches and always cried out for a bite. Those moments were precious, and each one lifted the grief a little more.

Each time Teresa received an afterlife sign, she felt a renewed sense of comfort. As the sharpness of the pain lessened, Teresa realized what a blessing it was to know without a doubt that her sweet girl was always nearby, and nothing would keep them apart.

Chapter 12

Electronic Signs

Electronic signs are easy to send because many of your daily activities are based around electronic or battery-operated devices.

I can turn the television on or off, change channels, or flicker the lights. I can set off smoke detectors with my presence or prompt devices to speak. There are so many ways to send electronic signs.

I am pure energy, so it is effortless to manipulate devices. I also can appear in your photos, especially in reflections, so check all the pictures you take. I love to push your buttons, so to speak, so if the remote control is acting up, you may not need new batteries, but you may have a visitor.

Next time something happens to one of your devices, ask for another sign to confirm it was me.

In the following story, a little dog with a big heart finds creative ways to send her mom a multitude of signs that all began with a photo on her smartwatch.

Chapter 13

Frankie

Frankie was a red apple head Chihuahua with a white spot on her back in the shape of a heart. Carolena rescued her as a puppy, and they spent the next thirteen years together. Everything changed when Frankie was diagnosed with diabetes and Cushing's disease.

Diabetes is challenging but manageable. When combined with Cushing's disease, things become more complicated.

Cushing's disease is usually caused by a tumor on the pituitary gland, and one of the first signs of the disease is excessive thirst.

Despite all the medication and treatments, Frankie showed no signs of improvement, and one day something was terribly wrong.

In a panic, Carolena rushed Frankie to the emergency vet clinic. They had to keep Frankie overnight and Carolena barely slept. The following day the vet called and said Frankie was having difficulty breathing.

When Carolena got in her car, an unexpected wave of peace washed over her, and time stood still. Within seconds, the doctor called and snapped her back to reality. When she heard the words, *Frankie passed away*, everything went silent.

The realization slowly came over her that Frankie had died alone around the exact time that wave of peace washed over her.

Carolena was spinning with so many thoughts. Maybe she wasn't supposed to see Frankie in her final moments. She wondered if the sense of peace that overcame her was a sign.

The immense pain that followed Frankie's transition was suffocating. Carolena cried for days and was unable to process simple thoughts. Desperate for relief she ordered a few books online about the afterlife of animals.

As she read more about the afterlife, she discovered that sometimes, companion animals go off alone when it is their time to leave. It is common in the animal kingdom to distance themselves during their final moments. Carolena began to realize that this was what was best for her and Frankie.

By accepting how things ended, Carolena started to sense Frankie's energy around her, which brought her so much comfort. Soon, even more unusual things happened around the house.

One day, Frankie's photo randomly appeared on Carolena's smartwatch. Her heart melted. For the first time since Frankie left, Carolena felt herself smile.

With renewed hope, Carolena asked Frankie for more signs. When the lights turned on by themselves, there was laughter and smiles. Soon, the television turned on by itself as well.

Although Frankie was very good at sending electronic signs, there were other types of signs too. Carolena was at the beach searching for seashells and didn't think to bring a shovel to dig in the sand.

A big wave knocked the bag of shells out of her hand. When the water receded, it revealed a small shovel buried in the sand. The signs were everywhere, and each one filled her heart with joy.

One day, Carolena was creating a business profile on social media. Frustrated by an error message that she could not fix, she decided to tackle the problem the next day and headed off to bed.

The next morning, she logged in and was baffled by a new post. It was a small brown dog with a red heart next to it. The post took her breath away. She had not published the page yet. No one could see the page or post on it. Carolena was the only one with access to that page. In disbelief, she stared at the photo and realized it was another electronic sign from Frankie.

Much to her surprise, cardinals began tapping on Carolena's windows. Another time she saw Frankie running through the house. Her other dog, Belle, was asleep on the sofa.

She also heard Frankie's distinctive sneeze when no one else was nearby. There were so many signs that it was hard to track them all. But one sign was truly unique.

When Carolena took a random photo in the house, there was an orb with the exact image of Frankie's face inside. An orb is a whitish-blue round anomaly that appears in photos that the naked eye cannot usually see. Soon, orbs with Frankie's face in them appeared in almost every picture she took.

Some signs appear in the most unexpected places. Carolena knows how Frankie likes sending signs, so she always looks for more. She is grateful for each one and always asks for more.

With hope restored, Carolena knows she and Frankie will always be connected. Each afterlife sign is a gift to be treasured, and her heart is full of love once more.

Chapter 14

Visual Signs

A visual sign is when you see part or all of me. Our worlds have aligned perfectly, and you can see into my dimension.

I may appear solid or transparent, and this is called manifesting. These visible signs are often fleeting, but that is due to the receptors in your eyes and brain.

Once our dimensions are out of alignment, I will begin to fade. I am still there. However, I am no longer in focus. You may see me in my bed or walking across the room. I may jump on or off the furniture or flash before your eyes.

Visual signs are real, and they will often surprise you. You may think it was your imagination or your eyes playing tricks on you.

These visible manifestations are not wishful thinking. We are on the same energetic wavelength for a brief moment in time.

Chapter 15

Bunny and Simba

Bunny

Simba

The house was so quiet without Bunny and Simba. Joan was all alone and deeply grieving the loss of her two cats. While mindlessly folding laundry, Joan noticed something out of place on the floor. She stepped closer to find a pure white feather. It was about two inches long and perfectly shaped. She burst into happy tears as a wave of love washed over her.

There was no logical explanation for the feather on the floor and she immediately sensed it was an afterlife sign. Joan had been asking for signs from Bunny and Simba and was about to get even more.

Bunny and Simba were littermates with the typical tabby coloring of black and brown stripes with the perfect letter M on their foreheads. Simba was a little whiter on his chest, and they both had beautiful green eyes.

Life did not start well for them. The kittens had been thrown from a moving vehicle and suffered serious injuries. Bunny's front leg was amputated and the road to recovery was long. Broken and abused, they needed someone to love them.

A friend told Joan that two kittens desperately needed a home. She and her husband, Mike, recently lost Max, their West Highland terrier. The house was sad and empty without him, so they were ready to welcome someone new. The timing was too coincidental to be ignored. Joan suspected that Max had something to do with sending the kittens to them. It was as if Max knew they were destined to be together.

Joan was even more convinced that it was not a coincidence when Bunny began behaving like Max. She sat in the same spot in the kitchen where Max always sat and displayed similar traits. Even though she was a kitten and Max was a dog, her mannerisms were like his.

The first indication that something was wrong was when Bunny was about sixteen and stopped using the litter box. Bunny was diagnosed with kidney disease. Despite all their efforts, Bunny's condition worsened, and Joan had to come to terms with an impossible decision. It was time to say goodbye to Bunny.

As heart-wrenching as it was, Joan felt Bunny knew it was her time to go. The timing was challenging because it was in the COVID-19 pandemic. The world was on lockdown, but Joan felt so fortunate that she could be with Bunny on her last day.

Many others could not be with their pets due to the pandemic. She thought how utterly devastating that must have been for them. With tears in her eyes, Joan held Bunny close and said goodbye to her sweet girl.

After Bunny transitioned, Joan kept her pain deep inside. Simba was grieving too. Without his lifelong companion, he was showing signs of depression and loneliness. The house felt sad and different without Bunny.

Six months later, they were struck with another terrible loss when Simba died from kidney failure at age seventeen. Simba had a tooth extracted and never fully recovered after that procedure.

Joan felt guilty about being so focused on Bunny that she may have let Simba's health slip through the cracks. Things might have been different if she had checked his kidney levels. With the residual grief from losing Bunny, Joan was now utterly lost.

Grief makes you question everything. Joan wondered if she had waited too long to let Simba go. Searching for answers, Joan found a grief support group and developed an interest in animal communication. She decided to grasp the idea of asking for signs, and it didn't take long before she received her first sign.

With this new perspective, Joan had a positive outlet to work through her feelings. Once she released the painful emotions, she felt more connected to Bunny and Simba. She celebrated all their happiest memories which kept their connection strong. That spurred more unexplainable events in the months ahead.

Bunny only had three legs and hopped like a rabbit, which is how she got her name. One day Joan saw an apparition of Bunny hopping through the kitchen and then vanishing into thin air. She also saw Simba from the corner of her eye as he went out the door. Joan was thrilled and excited to know Bunny and Simba's energy was still with her.

Joan continues to ask for afterlife signs and has allowed healing into her heart. She moved through the pain from her losses and in time, restored balance, and happiness in her life once more.

Chapter 16

Daisy

It was destiny that brought Keith and Daisy together. A random moment in time when Keith was on his way home one night. At the last minute, he decided to turn down a side street and stop at the local grocery store.

Up ahead, he saw the flashing lights of a police vehicle on the side of the road. As he drove closer, he saw a white dog being held down by someone.

The dog raised her head and made eye contact with Keith. He had no idea whose dog it was or what had happened. He slowly made his way past the police vehicle and headed home. After he arrived home, he could not stop thinking about that dog.

The following day Keith awoke and felt compelled to find her.

From the moment they made eye contact, something resonated within him. He called local veterinary offices, hoping to track her down. It didn't take long before he found her. The second veterinary office confirmed she was there.

The news was not good.

They informed him that the dog had been hit by a car and suffered a broken leg. The dog's owner did not want to spend the money on surgery. They were going to euthanize her that morning.

Keith's heart jumped. He couldn't let that happen and frantically told them not to euthanize her and that he was on his way. He bolted out the door to save her from certain death.

The owners signed the dog over to him without hesitation, and Keith rushed her to a specialist for the urgent medical care she needed.

Daisy was a thirty-pound American Eskimo mix with medium-length white wavy fur. She made it through the surgery but was scared and confused when Keith brought her home.

Keith slept on the floor with her at night to comfort her and ease her anxiety. He wanted Daisy to know that she was safe and that this was her forever home.

As time passed and Daisy's wounds healed, she began to trust Keith. Soon she followed him everywhere and loved to sit next to him in his chair. Their bond grew so strongly that she knew his routine. Like clockwork, at 3:00 pm every day, she looked out the front window waiting for him to come home from work.

Keith decided to rescue another dog as a companion for Daisy. Fonzie was a black schnauzer mix, and they instantly bonded.

As the years passed, Daisy struggled with mobility issues. Keith built ramps for her and carried her up and down the stairs to help ease her arthritis. One day she fell off the sofa and could not stand up, so Keith made an appointment at the veterinary clinic.

They had to run tests, so Keith left her there, hoping to pick her up later that day. When the call came in, the news was disturbing and completely unexpected. Daisy was in kidney failure and within a short time, passed away.

Keith was devastated that he could not be there with Daisy. He felt empty and lost without her. In the depths of pain, he and Fonzie comforted each other as they mourned their loss.

The first night after Daisy transitioned, Keith woke up with a jolt.

He opened his eyes and saw Daisy in her favorite spot at the foot of his bed.

She was solid, life-sized, and looked so happy just watching him.

He thought for sure he was hallucinating.

He jumped up, startled and bewildered, not knowing what to do.

Daisy instantly vanished, but he was sure it was real and not a dream.

Daisy appeared again the next night as well, and many more visitations would come in the weeks ahead.

Keith was curious about his vision, so he searched online for answers. He was elated to discover that the apparition he saw was a real manifestation.

Daisy let him know she would always be there by his side. He felt great comfort and for the first time his pain lessened.

Along with those appearances, Keith heard Daisy's distinctive snore and felt her lying beside him several times. He caught another glimpse of her, which looked like a transparent outline of her head as she ran across the floor.

Another time, he saw Daisy sitting in the dog bed. The apparitions never lasted long, but it was her.

When he got his new puppy, Teddy, he noticed he had many of the same traits as Daisy. He sleeps in the same spot on the sofa and looks out the window just like she did.

Keith has a new sense of peace and comfort. He watches for new signs and trusts that Daisy is always by his side.

He knows Daisy came into his life because he was lonely. Her loving soul filled an emptiness he did not know he had.

Destiny brought them together on that fateful day on the side of the road, and the bonds of love keep them connected for eternity.

Chapter 17

Imprinting

Imprinting is when my energy merges with yours and forms into a thought. I may imprint an idea, an image, an emotion, or flashes of our favorite memories.

A message instantly pops into your mind, and you think of me. It may bring a wave of emotions or tears but can also remind you of happier times.

These impressions come through clearly when your mind is quiet, or you are doing something neutral such as brushing your teeth, driving down a familiar road, doing the dishes, or sitting quietly.

You may think it is your thought, but it is my presence you are sensing. Our energy merges and you can easily intercept my thoughts

In the following story, you will discover how an imprinted message from a Labrador retriever foretold a sudden and unexpected loss.

Chapter 18

Rainey

Patty's mind wandered while she drove to work one day. She was not thinking about anything when she heard a clear voice.

Mom, it's okay. I'm in a beautiful place, and I'm happy.

Patty snapped into focus. She instantly knew it was Rainey. Their black Labrador retriever had recently transitioned, and she and her husband, Kevin, were deeply grieving.

The voice was so loving and joyful. It just came to her and imprinted into her own thoughts.

Patty was so relieved and felt a huge weight lifted off her shoulders. She had been struggling to understand why Rainey's life ended so young. It bothered her to think that maybe Rainey was not ready to go. Hearing her message was such a comfort. The feeling of peace transformed the deep pain in her heart.

This was not the first time Rainey imprinted her thoughts on Patty. A few weeks earlier, Patty had seen a look on Rainey's face that she would never forget.

Rainey was usually a ray of sunshine, but something was not right. Patty could not pinpoint what might be wrong — an ominous feeling imprinted upon her.

One morning, Rainey followed Patty through her daily routine and farm chores. Everything seemed fine so Patty brushed off the unsettling thoughts she had earlier.

The next day, tragedy struck when Rainey unexpectedly became paralyzed, and they had to say goodbye.

Rainey collapsed while she was with Patty's husband, Kevin. In a panic, they rushed her to the vet clinic, and the test results revealed the source of the paralysis. A slipped disc in her spine paralyzed her hind legs.

Surgery to replace the degenerative disc was the only option but there were no guarantees it would be effective. Rainey was only eight years old and could easily reinjure her spine or never regain mobility. Through their tears, they realized saying goodbye was the best decision for Rainey.

Patty was not prepared for the grief that ensued. She had always thought she was strong until the day Rainey was gone. She was convinced that the love she shared with Rainey had to be somewhere. Something as substantial as their love could not simply disappear.

In her quest for answers, Patty discovered more about the afterlife and how departed companions were always nearby. That realization was pivotal in her healing journey.

Patty began to honor Rainey and acknowledge her presence. That decision opened a door that grief had shut. Patty trusted Rainey was near and asked for signs.

One night, she felt Rainey jump off her bed. She was sure it was not her other dog, Redy. When it happened a second time, she realized it was another sign, and her heart filled with joy.

Patty thanked Rainey for the beautiful visit and asked for more. She began to feel close to Rainey again, and in that closeness, another sign appeared.

Patty got up one night to let Redy outside before bed. All the lights were off, but as Patty walked through the darkened house, a beam of light began shining over her shoulder. She turned around and saw the light shining on a picture of Rainey on the wall. It was the only picture in the spotlight.

When Patty realized how blessed she was to be the chosen caretaker of all her companion animals, she let go of the grief. This new perspective helped her so much when her beloved horse transitioned. By celebrating their bond, Patty felt more balanced and less focused on the pain.

Her experience with Rainey lifted Patty to a higher level of awareness. Rainey had a purpose for being with her, which gave Patty a new outlook on life and the afterlife.

She is more present with her animal companions and nurtures each relationship. She cherishes her role as caretaker and has found a new depth of love she never thought she would have again.

Life on the farm has transformed into a loving and happy place, and Patty has moved from despair to a calm and peaceful life.

Chapter 19

Physical Touch Signs

Physical touch signs are when you feel my fur brush against you or the warmth of my body next to you.

I may lick your face, your hand, or your toes. I long for your touch just as you long for mine, so don't be surprised if you feel my fur brush against you.

I may lie next to you so you can feel the warmth of my spirit body. I might even bump you with my paw or nose or climb in your lap.

Physical touch signs are thrilling because you know that you felt something.

My daily routine includes following you or spending time in my favorite spots. So even if you move to another home, don't worry, I will follow you wherever you go.

Physical touch signs are incredibly powerful as you are about to discover in the following story. A cat named Lola makes her presence known through a multitude of signs.

Chapter 20

Lola

After sixteen years together, Vicki said goodbye to her beloved gray cat, Lola. Overwhelmed with grief, she ordered a stone memorial for her burial site. Vicki wanted something beautiful to honor her sweet girl. Vicki was thrilled when the memorial stone finally arrived.

"Lola! Lola!" Vicki said out loud, "Your stone arrived!"

Vicki grabbed her keys and went to the door to get the

package. She heard something metallic hit the ground. She looked at the floor and saw a charm from her key chain.

She picked it up and could not believe her eyes. It was a charm in the shape of a cat. A rush of emotions washed over Vicki. It was the first of many signs she would receive from her green-eyed girl.

Lola was a quiet and dignified cat, yet she could be silly too. Her antics always brought a smile to Vicki's face. When Lola lost her appetite, Vicki took her for a senior check-up. The test results revealed a thyroid imbalance and the onset of kidney disease.

Since Lola had been healthy her entire life, Vicki was not overly concerned. But as time passed, Lola's health continued to decline. Despite the new medication, Lola was not herself.

Vicki sat on the floor one day and gazed into those green eyes. It pained her to know Lola was not feeling well. Vicki realized Lola might be ready to go. Her spark was no longer there.

"Lola, is it your time?" Vicki asked with tears falling down her face. "What do you want me to do? Are you done here?"

Lola sat quietly, watching Vicki. The answer came to Vicki immediately. It was like her own thought, but she knew it was Lola. It was time to say goodbye. A flood of emotions overcame her and through her tears.

Vicki promised to help her leave her body. The weight lifted once the decision was made, and Vicki sensed she had made the best decision.

Their time together came to an end so quickly. Vicki questioned everything she did and didn't do for Lola. Blurred from the pain, she could barely function. The guilt was unbearable and left her in a dark emotional void. She buried Lola in the backyard and prayed for a sign she was okay.

Vicki believed departed pets go to a heavenly place and she was determined to find out more. When she discovered that Lola's energy was still alive in the afterlife, she began to receive signs.

One night, as Vicki fell asleep, she saw Lola's profile beside her. Vicki watched in amazement as Lola casually walked to the end of her bed and vanished. She looked as natural as if she were still alive.

Vicki had no other cats, so knowing Lola was still with her was comforting and exciting. At that moment, Vicki felt all the guilt start to melt away.

As Vicki awoke from a deep sleep one morning, she saw Lola. As Vicki petted her soft fur, Lola licked her thumb with her raspy tongue. Lola walked over to her as Vicki continued to pat her gently. She felt Lola's paws as she stepped on her to continue to the other side of the bed.

The entire experience was so realistic. Vicki opened her eyes and Lola was gone, but when she closed her eyes, she saw Lola again. Vicki was thrilled when this happened and thanked her for this beautiful visit.

The more Vicki learned about the afterlife, the more she realized everything that happened was part of their story. Slowly, she began to forgive herself and let go of the grief. The challenges they faced were part of the journey for spiritual growth. Even loss was just another chapter in their story.

The signs from Lola continued to appear. Vicki heard unexplainable scratching sounds from Lola's bed. Her photo magically appeared on her phone, and she saw an unexplained movement out of the corner of her eye. Songs often play when she thinks about her, especially the songs *You Are My Sunshine* and *Lola*.

Vicki embraced the fact that the soul lives on, and each experience brought more peace and comfort. Their deep connection opened her eyes to the unlimited possibilities of their eternal connection and allowed her to move forward on her healing journey.

Chapter 21

Dreams

Dream visitations are vivid, emotionally intense interactions of our souls while you sleep. Unlike regular dreams, these nightly visits are realistic, memorable and change you forever.

They are often infused with powerful messages or loving insights. When you are asleep, your mind relaxes, making it much easier for me to get a message through to you.

While you are awake, daily distractions and mind chatter may block my messages. However, I can easily connect with you while you sleep.

Dream visits are so meaningful that you will wake up looking for me and know without a doubt that you held me or felt my presence.

Dream visitations are always beautiful, loving and uplifting.

You will feel joyous and peaceful during our energetic reunion. You will have a new understanding and an acceptance that may have escaped you before.

You and I are limitless during a dream visit, soaring through the clouds together. You get to experience how effortless it is to be in my dimension.

We will most likely exchange loving telepathic messages during our visit. So basically, we speak without saying a word and feel the incredible intensity of our love.

There will also be many dream visits from me that you do not remember. Just because you don't remember your dreams does not mean I am not visiting you.

Many factors are involved with why some people remember dreams while others do not. The stress from losing me is powerful and may cause you not to remember your dreams.

If you cannot remember your dreams, get a journal, and keep it beside your bed. As soon as you wake up, write down as many dreams as you can recall.

It may take some time, but the more you take notes, the easier it will be to remember your dreams.

Bad dreams are not visitations,

just subconscious thoughts surfacing while you sleep.

Bad dreams happen to everyone. Most of the time, those dreams are subconscious thoughts playing out different scenarios while you sleep. It is not a visitation if you have a bad dream about me.

The subconscious mind is the part of you that never rests. It records events day and night, and when you experience a loss, stress, grief, or anxiety, all those things accumulate and can contribute to nightmares or night terrors.

Certain medications or substances can also contribute to disturbing dreams. If you wake up and feel sad, restless, or fearful, remember the afterlife is loving, peaceful, and safe.

I am never in pain or in any danger.

I never experience any of the crazy things in your nightmares. So let go of anything like that and trust it was just a bad dream.

Place a note under your pillow inviting me to visit.

The best way to have a dream visit from me is to invite me to join you before you go to sleep. Place the note under your pillow or beside the bed. As you fall asleep, set your intention to meet me on a higher plane of awareness.

Dream visits symbolize our soul connection and how we are all spiritual beings having a physical experience. We do not need a body to love each other.

I may come to you in a dream if you need to be reminded that the soul never dies, and we are eternal. Dream visitations will open your heart to feel the power of our love once again.

Chapter 22

Fuzz

One night, Kerry had a vivid dream about her departed cat Fuzz. He walked toward her, radiating with happiness.

A few days later, she had another dream of an angel or a being of light holding Fuzz. She sensed he was letting her know he was loved and cared for, and everything was okay.

Fuzz was telling her to let go of painful thoughts.

Kerry woke up crying the happiest tears for the first time since he transitioned.

The guilt that followed his last day was intense. Fuzz was a thirteen-year-old cat with medium-length black fur. He had fluffy white fur around his neck and white whiskers, and his paws looked as if they were dipped in white paint.

At first, Kerry thought he was a stray but soon realized he lived across the street at her neighbor's house. Fuzz had the brightest yellow eyes. He loved to climb up your leg and greet you with a hug. He was affectionate and vocal, and soon, he began spending more time with Kerry and her family.

Over time the neighbors agreed Fuzz had chosen a new family and allowed them to keep him. He got along great with everyone, including Kerry's other pets. Kerry and Fuzz were inseparable. They had an inexplicable connection, and he was always by her side.

One day, Kerry noticed something was not quite right with Fuzz. He had been losing weight over the last few months, and she initially thought it was a sign of old age.

When Fuzz stopped eating, Kerry had a sickening feeling that something was wrong. Kerry took him to the veterinary clinic, and they discovered Fuzz was in the final stages of kidney failure. Kerry and her family were heartbroken.

Fuzz's once bright eyes became dull. It was clear he was not doing well. The daily fluids and appetite stimulants were not enough to keep him going. Kerry carried him around like a baby, tending to his every need. Fuzz loved being held, and those last days together were precious. At eighteen years of age, his body was shutting down.

Kerry had never had to euthanize a companion before, and it seemed so horrible despite his failing health. She made the appointment and took Fuzz to the clinic with her nine-year-old son. They held him close and found it hard to find the right words to say goodbye.

Everything was calm until the doctor administered the lethal injection. Fuzz suddenly leaped out of her arms in pain.

Kerry was horrified and desperately tried to soothe him. The injection stung as it entered the bloodstream.

Within minutes, Fuzz was gone, and his adverse reaction to the injection left a deep scar in her heart.

They carried Fuzz out to the car to bury him at home. When she drove out of the clinic, the first song on the radio was *Memories, by Maroon Five.* The touching lyrics about grief and losing someone you loved filled her with a wave of emotions.

Kerry desperately wanted to know if Fuzz was okay. She hoped he understood they were trying to help him. She sought relief from the intense pain by researching the afterlife of animals. Kerry ordered a few books and was fascinated by signs from the afterlife.

Kerry believed their love was so strong that nothing could keep them apart, and she was right.

Soon Fuzz appeared around the house. Kerry saw him in his favorite places by the food bowl and the door. They were fleeting images, but they brought her so much comfort.

Those visual manifestations led to physical visitations where Kerry felt him as he jumped off the bed. Her other cats were nowhere to be seen, so she knew it was Fuzz.

When Kerry focused on strengthening her connection with Fuzz, everything started to shift. She slowed down to be more present and in the moment. She found that sadness and swirling endlessly in grief took her away from what was happening around her, so she shifted her focus to be more positive.

Kerry realized she could direct her feelings in a more productive way that would also help Fuzz on his journey.

Over time, the overwhelming pain lifted. She embraced her emotions and never lost hope. She relied on her support system of loved ones and others who have lost a beloved companion to move forward.

As Kerry developed her intuition, the more signs and visits she received.

Her heart opened with a new sense of life and the afterlife. Kerry honored her feelings and moved forward into healing, knowing that Fuzz will always be nearby.

Chapter 23

Rex

One night, Melissa had a dream that was unlike any other. Her Chihuahua, Rex, was on her lap, and she felt his fur. Rex nuzzled her, and a wave of happiness washed over her.

Her dream was so vivid she expected to see him when she opened her eyes in the morning.

Rex was Melissa's best friend and a grounding force in her busy world. They took long walks together, and he was always with her. He was sweet, affectionate, and loved to cuddle.

When they were together, the demands of Melissa's hectic schedule as a nurse and mom melted away. She called him her *King*, and her world revolved around him.

Rex was large for the breed, weighing twelve pounds. Despite his large size, the DNA results confirmed he was a hundred percent purebred. Rex had a sable-colored coat and was ten weeks old when Melissa brought him home.

With her medical background, Melissa noticed the telltale signs of liver issues when Rex was about nine. Symptoms can vary but include a swollen belly, vomiting, lethargy, and yellowing or jaundice of the eyes, gums, or tongue.

Melissa was overcome with the onset of anticipatory grief.

Those around us often misunderstand anticipatory grief and the impact it has. Rex was still alive, but anticipating his loss triggered an unexpected storm of emotions.

A check-up at the veterinarian's office confirmed her worst fears. Rex was in liver failure. Melissa did her best to keep him comfortable, but his condition worsened. The doctor recommended euthanasia, and Melissa realized it was the only option. She held Rex gently in her arms and whispered goodbye. Her *King* took his last breath on his tenth birthday.

As Melissa began the slow journey through grief, she searched online for anything to comfort her broken heart.

She listened to audiobooks while taking walks and soon discovered more about the afterlife. She started to say Rex's name to draw him closer. She found a support group and found it helpful to share her story with others who had lost a beloved companion.

Melissa spoke to Rex daily and shared everything that had happened to her. She told him how much she missed him and wished he was near. She told him about the squirrels, rabbits, and birds she saw on her walks.

Knowing Rex heard her words gave her great comfort. Many tears fell during those walks, but Melissa's pain lifted a little more with each step.

As the days passed, Melissa kept their connection alive by paying attention to her surroundings. His love taught her how to be more patient and in the moment.

She watches for signs and keeps a positive outlook. With Rex's energy by her side, Melissa opened her heart and discovered that true love never ends.

Chapter 24

Audible Signs and Sounds

Audible signs are when you hear me or the noises I make.

These sounds may be fleeting, but they are obvious.

Maybe you heard a bark or meow or a whine or cry.

Maybe you heard a sneeze or snore or the sound of my nails on the floor.

I may scratch the carpet or the wall or go through the doggy door.

You may hear my collar or the sound of me breathing.

These signs are exciting for both of us, and you may think it is your imagination, but it is not. Your higher self knows it is me, and in that brief moment, we are once again sharing the same space at the same time.

I will never send you any distress sounds. It is impossible to be in distress in the afterlife. Distress sounds may be residual loops of energy that your mind taps into.

These energy loops can be unnerving, but I promise that they are not me.

There are many frequencies you cannot hear without special equipment. But sometimes, unexplained things happen, and you hear something. I do not know how it works or why, but unknown phenomena are part of our world, and there is so much we have yet to learn.

Audible signs from me will be filled with happiness and excitement as you are about to discover in this next story.

Chapter 25

William

A large nine-year-old black dog was surrendered to the shelter by his family. He was part Labrador retriever with a little bit of Great Dane, German shepherd, and a touch of wolf. He was in rough shape and suffered from parasites, fungal bacteria, and infections on his skin. He weighed ninety-six pounds and had extreme separation anxiety. He was shutting down in the stressful shelter environment. Someone needed to help him.

Karen's daughter was involved with rescue groups and thought her mom was the perfect match for this gentle giant. Without hesitating, Karen brought William home for some much-needed tender loving care. She had fostered other dogs, so this was not the first time a shelter dog wiggled a way into her heart.

It took a long time before Will became stable, but as a nurse, Karen was determined and prepared to help him. She worked on his separation anxiety for months, and he eventually reached the point where she could leave the house without him launching into a panic.

Will followed her everywhere and would do anything to be by her side. He once climbed through an open window to be with her. Will had many talents, including opening a deadbolt lock with his teeth and letting himself outside. Once he realized Karen loved him and would never leave him, he finally relaxed and settled down.

The bond that grew between them was remarkable. There are some companions that have a profound and unexplainable effect on our lives and Will did just that. It is hard to describe unless you have experienced it yourself.

Every day was a joy and as much as Karen helped Will, he enriched her life too. She was honored to have such a loyal and loving connection.

When Will was almost fourteen, he began to show signs of aging. His rear legs started to give out and he tired easily. It became clear that his time to leave was looming.

Karen decided to do something special for Will before she said goodbye. To honor their amazing connection, she knighted him *Sir William of Karen*. His new role was the greeter on the Rainbow Bridge. The Rainbow Bridge is a mythical heavenly place where many believe their animals wait for them to be reunited.

The veterinarian arrived and Karen got on the floor next to Will. With tears in her eyes, she told him how much she loved him and how he had changed her life forever. His soulful brown eyes were filled with gratitude. He reached up and gave her one last kiss. He laid his head down, took a deep breath, and was gone.

Will left this world knowing he was special and very loved.

After Will transitioned the emptiness was crushing. Finding her way through the emotional turmoil was so hard but Will would soon make his presence known in a unique way.

Shortly after he passed, Karen heard Will's distinctive barks several times. Surprised and delighted, they were undeniably from him. There was no one else around yet Karen clearly heard him bark and it was like music to her ears. A wave of emotions washed over her knowing he was near. Time stood still as the magic of the moment embraced her.

Their time together was purposeful in countless ways. Will gave back every ounce of love Karen bestowed upon him and so much more. His devotion to her never ended. Karen found peace and comfort knowing she did the best she could for Will and continues to honor his memory without regrets.

Chapter 26

Lisa Kiddio

Kristina was home alone one night, grieving the loss of her cat, Lisa Kiddio, when she asked for a sign—anything to let her know that her beloved kitty was okay.

Suddenly, she heard footsteps on her roof. Kristina froze. It was dark out, and there was no reason for anyone to be on the roof. She rushed outside to investigate, but no one was there.

Kristina asked a neighbor who was outside if anyone was on her roof. He did not see anything either. Then it hit her. She had just asked for a sign. A wave of emotions washed over her as she realized it was Lisa Kiddio letting her know she was near. Kristina's heart swelled with joy.

The first time Kristina saw the young stray tabby in her yard, she assumed the cat belonged to a neighbor. The kitty was very friendly, and Kristina tried to find the owners, but no one claimed her. Kristina had never had a cat, but there was something about this affectionate little girl and she welcomed her into her life.

Kristina named her Lisa Kiddio because she liked the name Lisa, and she acted like a silly kid. Her new companion followed her everywhere and especially loved to be in the garden.

Her black, brown, and gray tiger stripes complimented her pale green eyes. Lisa Kiddio was playful and intelligent and understood words in English and Swedish, Kristina's native language.

Many years later, Kristina noticed Lisa Kiddio started losing weight and was not sleeping in her usual places. At sixteen years, she thought it was just the onset of aging, but

Kristina took her to the veterinarian clinic for a check-up. The blood tests revealed that Lisa Kiddio had kidney disease.

Kristina was crushed and could not imagine life without her best friend. They had become so close over the years. She decided to celebrate their remaining time and not waste a single breath on anything negative.

Kristina doted on Lisa Kiddio daily and catered to everything she needed. Everything Kristina did centered around her. The bond between them grew even stronger and she cherished every moment. Despite her attentive, loving care, kidney disease took its toll on Lisa Kiddio. Kristina knew it was time.

On their last night together, Kristina snuggled beside Lisa Kiddio and held her departed grandmother's photo. She asked her grandmother to greet her beloved girl when she died. Lisa Kiddio's condition worsened the following day, and Kristina made the impossible decision and said her final goodbye to her beloved girl.

The pain from the loss of Lisa Kiddio was immense. The house had never felt so empty. Desperate to find relief from the pain, Kristina searched online for answers about the afterlife and by doing so, discovered animal communication.

Fascinated by this new concept of understanding the animals, Kristina dove in to learn as much as possible. At first, she developed her intuitive skills with the sole purpose of communicating with Lisa Kiddio. Once she realized how life-changing it was to receive a message, she started conducting sessions for others who had lost a beloved companion.

Kristina learned how departed companions send signs from the afterlife such as the footsteps she heard on her roof. It was all so amazing and profoundly healing. The more she learned about the afterlife the more her broken heart healed.

Receiving messages from the animals allowed Kristina to focus her energy in a positive way. Departed companions shared detailed messages as if they were still alive and well.

The experience was fascinating and illuminated Kristina's world in an unexpected way. The little stray cat that came into her life was the catalyst for spiritual growth in so many beautiful ways. Kristina knows that Lisa Kiddio's presence is always near guiding her on this new and incredible path.

Chapter 27

Lucy

Nicole was awakened by the distinctive sound of Lucy's bark. She was not dreaming. It was a real bark. It was so loud she sat up in bed and looked for Lucy. Her two other dogs were sound asleep, and their barks were softer and not so intense. The opposite of Lucy's strong voice. Nicole was thrilled and felt a wave of goosebumps and excitement envelop her. She finally got a sign that her sweet girl was still with her.

Lucy was very vocal when she was alive, so it made sense that she was just as communicative in the afterlife. The sense of joy and relief was instant. Finally, the fog from grief lifted. Lucy was still with her.

Lucy came into her life as an eight-week-old yellow American Labrador retriever puppy. American Labrador retrievers are bred to be leaner and have longer legs than the more common English Labrador retrievers. Lucy was a funny girl, full of life, and she loved to play with Nicole's children.

One of Lucy's favorite things to do was to bark as loud as possible in the car. Her barks were so abrupt they startled Nicole every time they went for a ride. She also barked loudly when she wanted her treats in an unmistakably demanding way.

Lucy also made quite a scene by cornering stink bugs in the yard and barking relentlessly at them. She could also be a little bit naughty. With a passion for stealing food, Lucy pulled an entire tray of Italian cannoli pastries off the table one day. Lucy had a stubborn side too. She would drop onto the floor and refuse to move if she didn't want to do something.

When Lucy was about nine years old, Nicole noticed some disturbing changes. Lucy was panting more than she should, losing weight, and urinating more frequently. After a check-up at the veterinary clinic, she was diagnosed with diabetes. They began a regimen of daily doses of insulin to maintain her glucose levels. Diabetes was challenging to regulate, but they were determined to do their best for their girl.

Despite diligent care, Lucy's condition worsened. She lost her eyesight overnight and began to have mobility issues. When they found a mass in Lucy's stomach, Nicole realized she had an impossible decision to make. The thought of one day without Lucy was agonizing, let alone the rest of her life. Sadly, the family gathered to say their goodbyes to their beautiful girl.

Lucy's absence left a vast emptiness in their home. The laughter and joy dissipated. They had two other small dogs, yet it felt far too quiet without Lucy's vibrant presence. Desperate for answers and guidance, Nicole searched online for anything she could find about the afterlife, grief, and pet loss. She hoped that death was not the end and there would be a way to know that Lucy was okay.

As she discovered more about the afterlife, Nicole felt closer to Lucy than ever before. It warmed her heart to know that Lucy felt the love she shared with her other dogs. The pain eased once Nicole discovered how Lucy would always be nearby. She found great comfort in knowing it was not the end for Lucy but just a change of dimensions.

Certain things can trigger emotions and tears, but Nicole has moved forward on a healing journey. Her beloved girl, Lucy, was by her side through many life events. Now she is confident that Lucy will remain right there, leaning into her with her whole body from the afterlife. Joy and laughter fill their home once again, and Nicole and her family look forward to welcoming a new puppy.

Chapter 28

Feathers, Whiskers, and Moving Objects

Objects are some of the most common signs I send. It may be a feather, a tuft of fur, or a whisker. You may find toys, treats, or other carefully placed objects in unusual places.

These signs can be anywhere you spend time or places you visit. There is often a surge of emotions when you find these unique signs. When that happens, it is your soul recognizing my energy around each object.

I can also move objects like doors, cupboards, or food bowls. The afterlife overlaps your world, so when the time is right, I can move those items as if I still have a body. I can also leave nose smudges on windows and doors to tell you I am always still with you.

Other objects can appear outside in nature. A stone, leaf, or flower may capture your eye. It may have a unique shape or color. An object sign will stand out from its surroundings, seem out of place, or be purposefully placed in your path.

I may send you an object sign once or hundreds of times. The frequency of these little surprises is based on my personality and the environment.

One object sign is just as significant as many. These are not coincidental discoveries. This is how we do things in the afterlife. We find creative ways to capture your attention and reassure you that we never left.

In the following chapter, a little dog sends a little feather after leaving a big impression on everyone he met.

Chapter 29

Lil' Roy

Sandy was at the stable one day, spending time with her horses. She had recently said goodbye to her beloved Lil' Roy, a white Pomeranian and poodle mix. Being near her horses brought comfort and helped ease her broken heart.

Losing Lil' Roy was one of her worst experiences, but Sandy shifted her focus from the pain to celebrating his life and enjoying his memory every day. He made such a huge impact on her life and that was far more important than focusing on the grief.

The stables were oddly quiet that day with no one else around. Sandy walked by the arena and noticed a clear hoof print in the sand. As she got closer, she saw something that caught her eye.

There was a white feather tucked in the center of the hoof print. It was so perfectly placed right where she would find it. There were no birds, just that single feather in front of her. Sandy was overwhelmed with emotions.

Sandy sensed that Lil' Roy's energy was still alive and vibrant. She knew that feathers are often a sign a departed loved one was near, and she immediately knew it was from him. They had an unbreakable bond that began twelve years earlier.

"I'm bringing home a puppy," Sandy told her husband over the phone one day. "What? I can't hear you. We must have a bad connection; see you in a bit."

Sandy promptly ended the call with a smile, pretending she could not hear his response. She knew he would object to a new puppy, but after their kids left home, she had bouts of empty nest syndrome. Besides, how could he not fall in love with such a cute little puppy?

Lil' Roy was very different from the other dogs Sandy had. At an early age, she sensed he was an old soul, wise beyond his years. He was far more interested in being with people than playing with toys. She enrolled him in a pet therapy class when he was older, and Lil' Roy graduated with flying colors.

The two made the perfect team visiting the residents in assisted living. His sweet face brought a smile to everyone he met. He loved to wear little outfits and posed for every photograph. He was doing what he loved and made so many people happy.

All Sandy had to say were the words, *care center* and he would jump up and get ready to be a therapy dog. They traveled around spreading sunshine and happiness to so many in need. It was a wonder that such a little dog could significantly impact so many people.

As he got older, Lil' Roy developed a vestibular disorder that caused him to tilt his head. He had slowed down quite a bit and spent more time napping than he had in the past.

Sandy sensed their time was limited so she cherished every moment they had.

It was the day after Christmas that everything changed. Lil' Roy suddenly passed away from heart disease. Sandy was heartbroken. The center of her world was gone.

Sandy had said goodbye to other companions before but managed the grief differently this time. *Love can continue,* she thought to herself. It is that powerful.

Shortly after he transitioned, Sandy realized that Lil' Roy's personality could not just disappear. She believed there was something more than our physical world. She wanted to believe Lil' Roy was still with her.

She found answers about the afterlife and read everything she could find about the topic. The stories helped her realize that Lil' Roy was just in a new dimension. It was all so fascinating, and Sandy wanted to learn how to access that space.

Above all, she didn't want to dwell on the sadness.

Sandy sharpened her skills and adjusted her perceptions to communicate more effectively with him. Once she left doubt behind, she accessed a whole new world.

The first signs from Lil' Roy were subtle yet unmistakable. Sandy made a necklace with his photo and a rainbow on it. When she took a picture of his memorial, a rainbow and a glowing light appeared above her.

She had a little stuffed doggie toy resembling Lil' Roy that suddenly disappeared. She searched everywhere and could not find it. The stuffed doggie mysteriously reappeared when she decided to bring a new puppy home. She knew it was a sign from Lil' Roy saying he approved of the new puppy.

Looking for afterlife signs helped Sandy move forward and gave her something to celebrate. Knowing Lil' Roy is alive and vibrant in his dimension motivated her to be a better mom to her new pups and horses.

She continues to receive signs from Lil' Roy, and her enthusiasm for every message is contagious. Sandy trusts their connection will continue, and she will someday look into Lil' Roy's soulful eyes again.

Chapter 30

Sweet Pea

The lobby of the emergency clinic was eerily quiet as the veterinarian technician whisked Sweet Pea into the back room. The clinic was usually crowded and noisy, but Artemis and her husband, Darryl, were the only ones there.

They anxiously sat in silence and waited for an update. Something was wrong with their beloved fifteen-year-old miniature schnauzer.

The night before, Sweet Pea started coughing and pacing around the house. She could not get comfortable. At the clinic, Sweet Pea was given oxygen to help her breathe, but the prognosis was bleak. Her heart had filled with fluid, and she was rapidly declining.

Artemis heard the terrible news, and instantly her heart sank. They were unprepared to say goodbye that day and never thought they would leave without Sweet Pea. They gently held her as she took her final breath.

Sweet Pea had the typical salt and pepper color of a miniature schnauzer with cream on her muzzle and legs. She was affectionate and loved to be carried around like a baby. She always posed for the camera and enjoyed the attention.

Highly intelligent, Sweet Pea understood hand signals and facial gestures and could easily read minds.

Even though Artemis had a solid support system, the loss of Sweet Pea was overwhelming. There were reminders everywhere around the house from all their years together, and the silence was deafening. Artemis was so lost without her. She spoke to her constantly, asking if she was okay and pleading for a sign.

Moving through grief was a struggle but the most significant part of her healing journey was when Artemis learned about the afterlife of animals. Once she discovered how animals send messages and signs, a new world opened for her.

With the support of like-minded people, Artemis found the crucial missing link to moving forward. The pain was always just beneath the surface, but ever so slowly, she found a path through the turmoil.

About two weeks after Sweet Pea transitioned, the first signs began to appear. Artemis was at a store and saw white feathers on the ground. Her heart skipped a beat because the feathers seemed placed right where she would see them. She immediately sensed it was an afterlife sign from Sweet Pea.

With new hope, she asked for another sign, and much to her surprise, she opened a closet door and found a decorative white dove she had forgotten about.

Artemis noticed the numbers ten and eleven appearing which was the date Sweet Pea transitioned, October 11th. One night after Artemis and Darryl went to bed, they heard scratching noises on the carpet. It was the same sound

Sweet Pea made as she nestled in for the night. No other pets were in the house, so they knew it was her.

A bright blue dragonfly flew up to Artemis and hovered for a long time as if to say *hello*. The signs continued and soon dream visits brought tremendous comfort to their broken hearts, and they were so grateful for each one. Sweet Pea was letting them know she was still a part of their life.

On the anniversary of Sweet Pea's transition, Artemis and Darryl honor her memory with balloons and a celebration and reminisce about their favorite moments. From the day they found her, it was as if, by some miracle, the Universe conspired, and they were meant to be together.

Artemis thinks about her precious girl, Sweet Pea, every day and focuses on the beautiful memories they made. They were destined for each other and remained connected for eternity.

Chapter 31

Bailey

Vicki needed a distraction from the grief of losing her Australian shepherd, Bailey, so she cleaned the house from top to bottom. She scrubbed and vacuumed furiously as the tears streamed down her face.

Desperate to escape the pain and sadness, the mindless task was something she could do to fill the enormous void that Bailey had left behind.

The next day, Vicki went into the spare room that was spotless the day before and noticed something on the carpet. On the floor where she thoroughly vacuumed were two tufts of Bailey's fur.

They had no other pets, so Vicki knew it was from Bailey. She burst into happy tears and was overcome with emotions. That obvious sign brought so much comfort, knowing Bailey was still there.

For the first time since she said goodbye, a feeling of peace soothed her broken heart.

Bailey, or Miss Bea as they often called her, was a blue merle with a black, gray, brown, and white coat. She was so well behaved she went to work every day with Vicki and her husband, Andy.

Bailey was quite popular at the jobsite, and everyone loved her. She was funny and intelligent too. When Bailey didn't get her way, she expressed her discontent by tipping the cat food bowl upside down.

When Bailey was about eleven years old, her health started to decline. It began when she had difficulty urinating, so they took her to the veterinary clinic for a check-up.

The test results confirmed Lyme disease. Lyme disease is an autoimmune disease caused by tick bites with many different symptoms, from painful joints to lameness and fatigue.

Further testing revealed more concerning news. Bailey had a tumor near her bladder, explaining why she had difficulty urinating. The diagnosis was transitional cell carcinoma, which was not easy to remove.

The surgical options were limited, and there were no guarantees the outcome would be successful. Bailey had slowed down quite a bit and was not acting like her usual happy self. With few choices left, Vicki and Andy did not want to put their sweet girl through extensive procedures that may not be successful.

They made the painful decision to say goodbye.

The next few weeks without Bailey were devastating and surreal. The house was so empty and lifeless without their girl. Vicki was trying to decide how to memorialize Bailey and considered getting a tattoo but could not decide on a design.

That night she dreamed about a tattoo with the letter B. That was the sign Vicki needed. Bailey clearly communicated her excitement and approval. Vicki got the B tattoo, which brings her so much comfort and joy.

Bailey continues to make her presence known around the house through her distinctive scent. Andy knows Bailey is there when he smells popcorn in his office. When she was alive, Bailey's paws smelled just like popcorn.

The signs continue to appear and each one is precious. Out of the blue, a butterfly fluttered around them, and they instantly felt a flood of emotions knowing it was a sign from Bailey.

Their memories together will never be forgotten and just as she was in life, loyal and devoted, Bailey's energy is right by Vicki and Andy's side in the afterlife.

Chapter 32

Number Signs

Number signs can be single digits or a sequence of numbers that may contain a specific meaning. You may see repeating numbers, often called angel numbers, like 111 or 777. Sometimes, another number is in the sequence, such as 1101. That is still a message and should not be ignored.

I may send the date you brought me home or the time of day I left this Earth or another important anniversary.

Number signs can be on license plates, mailboxes, clocks, the change you receive, or the amount you pay for something. You may see a combination of numbers such as 07 and 22 which can be a birthday, such as July 22nd. Even if you see the numbers in reverse order, they still contain messages.

If you receive a lot of number signs, be sure to research numerology. Numerology is the belief that mystical or divine connections with numbers exist and influence your life and events.

Number signs are always intriguing, and in the following story, odd events occurring around the same day could only be explained as signs from the afterlife.

Chapter 33

Ralph & Oscar

Ralph (left) and Oscar (right)

The 25th of February was one of the saddest days Karen had ever known. Her white Maltese/poodle mix, named Ralph, made his transition at the age of fifteen. It also happened to be her other dog, Oscar's birthday.

Oscar was also a Maltese/poodle mix, and they looked like twins, except Oscar was a little bit bigger than Ralph. After that tragic day when Karen said goodbye to Ralph, a series of inexplicable events began to occur on or around the 25th of the month.

Karen had no idea that this was just the beginning of what could only be attributed to a multitude of signs from the afterlife. Too many odd things were happening for it to be a mere coincidence.

Ralph was exactly what Karen needed after her daughter left for college. They spent every moment together exploring the beaches and the new neighborhood. Ralph filled many voids in her life, and she loved doting on him and caring for his every need.

Oscar came into their lives when Karen decided that Ralph needed a friend. The two dogs were so cute together and they bonded immediately.

As the years passed by, Ralph began to suffer from recurring seizures. For months, Karen did everything she could, including daily trips to the veterinarian.

She devoted every waking moment to her dogs, and they became the center of her world. It was a helpless feeling when Ralph had seizures and over time, it took an emotional toll on all of them.

On his last day, Ralph had another seizure, so Karen rushed him to the veterinary office. By the time they arrived, Ralph was gone. The shock and pain were indescribable. Karen brought Ralph home for a backyard burial, overwhelmed with grief.

She found solace in Oscar's company. Oscar was deeply affected by the loss of Ralph, too, grieving for his friend and lifelong companion.

Shortly after Ralph transitioned, Karen noticed various animals started to appear in her yard. A series of creatures of all sizes made their presence known or peered in her windows.

A raccoon visited the backyard one day and calmly approached Karen's sliding glass door showing no signs of concern with her presence.

Another time, a big green lizard perched on the wall next to the window and gazed at Karen as if trying to get her attention. Not long after that, a small turtle wandered onto her backyard patio.

What was so strange about that turtle was the yard was surrounded by a block wall and there was no way this tiny visitor could have crawled over or under the wall.

Brightly colored birds perched just outside Karen's window and looked in, unafraid of her presence. As Karen documented these strange visits, they all occurred on or around the twenty-fifth of the month, the date Ralph passed away.

A year later, Oscar was diagnosed with cancer. After a toxic reaction to the treatments, he finally responded well to his new medication, and Karen savored every day they had left.

When Oscar's last moments were upon them, Karen could not help but notice the date on the calendar. It was the 26th of June.

She arranged for the veterinarian to come to her home to say her final goodbye. She cradled Oscar gently in her arms with tears in her eyes. The compounded loss of her beloved companions was the worst pain Karen had ever endured.

After a sleepless night and numbness from grief, Karen got up the next morning and thought a cup of coffee would help clear her mind. In the kitchen, she saw a reflection on the shiny porcelain floor. She rubbed her eyes in disbelief as an image appeared before her.

Both dogs appeared on the surface of the flooring. The unmistakable outline of Ralph and Oscar side by side was before her.

Fascinated by her experience, Karen began researching the signs from the afterlife and animal communication. Once she realized that their souls lived on, more signs appeared.

She found seashells and stones shaped like hearts. One night, she heard someone jump off the bed, just like Oscar used to do.

A swarm of dragonflies surrounded her in a choreographed dance, where she and Oscar walked several weeks before he transitioned.

Cloud formations looked just like them, and when she asked for more signs, doves appeared twice.

Karen saw butterflies, ladybugs, and feathers in odd places, and light bulbs went out for no reason. There were so many signs; each brought a flood of joy and comfort.

There were many days Karen thought she would never come out of the darkness. The crucial shift occurred when she decided to live in gratitude instead of grief. She allowed herself to move forward slowly at her own pace, with grace.

Even though she did not think she would get another dog, a post on social media changed her mind. Teddy was a malnourished stray who needed a second chance. He looked just like Ralph and Oscar, who likely had something to do with bringing Teddy into her life.

Karen makes a concerted effort to live fully in the moment and not dwell on the sorrow of the past. The timely odd occurrences keep happening and always bring a smile to her face. Teddy helped her through the pain and heartbreak and opened a new space for peace and healing in her heart.

Chapter 34

New Pet Signs

One of the fastest ways I can fill your heart with more love is to send a new companion to you.

There is a magical exchange of energy when someone new opens your heart. All those feelings that are bottled up inside are released, and little by little, the sun shines on your soul again.

It may take a while before you are ready. That is okay.

The thought of enduring another loss may be too much for you right now, so whenever you are ready, I may send someone special your way.

A new love in your life can help you through the pain and loneliness after a loss. Seeing you laugh, smile, and love again is my joy.

I am never concerned with being replaced. That is a human concept. There is enough love in the afterlife and from you to complete me.

Jealousy doesn't exist in spirit form, so never concern yourself with that. Life is meant to be lived joyfully and a new companion may be the best thing that ever happened to both of you.

It is a selfless act to adopt a new friend or give a stray a second chance in life. Some of the most magical connections are made when you open your heart to help someone in need.

The transformation you both experience is priceless.

Chapter 35

Transformations

A transformation is when you release old thoughts, patterns, or beliefs, shift into a more positive mindset, and pursue your dreams.

Perhaps you decide to live with more purpose, joy, or laughter. Maybe you are inspired to pursue a hobby, career, or other goal that has never been a priority. It is never too late to add joy to your life. Every second counts.

The possibilities are endless when you transform your life. No one arrives in the afterlife saying, *I wish I didn't spend so much time doing the things I love.* The exact opposite is true.

Many humans arrive with the heaviness of the world upon their shoulders. They worked too hard for too long and did not make their goals a priority.

Every day is a new opportunity to transform. You can do it. I will be right by your side every step of the way.

Get ready to be inspired. In the following stories, traumatic situations are transformed into a life with purpose.

Chapter 36

Kuba

When Jarka's black and white short-haired cat named Kuba came inside the house one day, she immediately sensed something was wrong. Jarka noticed a wound on his hip, but she had no idea what caused it. She rushed him to the veterinary clinic.

Kuba loved to be outside and never wandered far from their home in the Czech Republic, so Jarka was not sure how he got injured. When the doctor called with an update she was stunned.

Kuba had been shot.

According to the doctor, someone shot him at close range, and the bullet was lodged inside him. Kuba's condition was unstable, so they kept him overnight to monitor him.

Horrified, she contacted law enforcement officials. They informed her that several other cats in the neighborhood had also been shot.

Jarka and her family put fliers around the area warning others to keep their cats indoors. They hoped the fliers would generate leads on a suspect or the shooter would see the fliers and stop shooting cats.

When Jarka arrived at the clinic the next day to check on Kuba, the doctor said he was not doing well. Despite their efforts, he was not going to survive.

A few days ago, Kuba was alive and well and so happy. It was surreal and Jarka watched helplessly with tears in her eyes as Kuba took his last breath.

A wall of pain descended upon Jarka thinking she had failed him. She felt guilty for not protecting him from harm. Her only comfort was being by his side for his last moments on Earth.

He left his body knowing he was loved.

As grief set in, she wondered if Kuba had waited for her to be there for his last breath.

The first few days after Kuba was gone were a blur for Jarka and her family. Facing the grim reality of a cat killer in the neighborhood was too much to bear. All Jarka wanted to do was sleep to stop the unavoidable pain.

As the days passed, Jarka thought about how Kuba waited for her. He passed so quickly after she arrived.

Thoughts swirled in her mind.

Maybe there was a purpose for this tragedy, but she had no idea what it could be.

Jarka found comfort by reading about afterlife signs. She realized that Kuba was trying to tell her something. Could it be that he waited for her to arrive at the clinic that day? Something inside clicked. He was part of her journey. Realizing there was a purpose for his loss was a crucial step forward through the darkness of grief.

That night, Jarka fell into a deep sleep for the first time since Kuba transitioned.

She relentlessly blamed herself for not protecting him, but now she realized it was not her fault, and she was not responsible for what happened.

Jarka released those feelings of guilt, and the inner turmoil began to subside.

Something inside her lit up.

A sense of knowing came over her.

Kuba was the spark she needed for the spiritual journey about to unfold.

Jarka enrolled in animal communication courses and found the process calming and powerfully enriching.

With her newly acquired skills, she catches glimpses of Kuba sitting peacefully in the yard soaking up the sun.

There are often unexplained footsteps in the house and the motion light sensor turns on for no reason.

Sometimes Kuba is so close, Jarka can feel his fur.

Jarka learned everything she could about the world of energy and afterlife communication. She understands how loved ones are always with us, and they want us to live a full and happy life.

Although they never found out who killed Kuba, no more shootings were reported.

Jarka pursued her dreams and is now a certified veterinary physiotherapist who relies on animal communication skills to help needy animals.

Kuba opened the space for Jarka to discover her natural intuitive abilities, and his tragic death had a higher purpose than anyone could imagine. He was the pivotal force in guiding Jarka to follow her true passion in life.

Chapter 37

Simon

Cassandra and Brian rescued Simon, a five-year-old Jack Russell terrier and Chihuahua mix, from a shelter in Massachusetts. He had short cream-colored fur with a hint of faded brown patches on his body and ears.

He was only about nine pounds, but he was affectionately known as their *Macho Man*. They bonded instantly and he went to work with her almost every day. Simon was loyal and protective yet loving and playful.

A routine visit to the veterinary clinic brought some troubling news. The doctors found a mass on Simon's heart and spleen. After surgery and treatment Simon did well for a while, but then he started to have seizures and was diagnosed with Cushing's disease.

Cassandra's greatest fear was losing him. She could not imagine one day without him. She was determined to keep their strong bond going no matter what happened.

As Simon's health deteriorated, Cassandra struggled with anticipatory grief, and often felt guilty if she did not spend enough time with him or when she became frustrated with his ongoing health issues.

Despite her efforts, the reality of the decision she had to make was becoming painfully clear. A massive seizure sent them back to the clinic in a panic. Cassandra and Brian prepared themselves for the worst.

The news was not good. It was time to say goodbye. As Cassandra cradled him gently in her arms, Simon took his last breath.

The grief and emptiness that followed were overwhelming and every decision about his health looped in her mind. Suddenly, Cassandra had a big breakthrough.

She realized she had faced her worse fear which was losing Simon. Facing that fear was empowering and gave her the strength to move forward despite her loss.

Cassandra started meditating and spent more time with her two other dogs, which was incredibly healing. Progress was slow, but she was determined to live a more meaningful life, and nothing would stop her. If she could face losing Simon, she could face anything in life.

Cassandra still awaits a sign, message, or dream but knows deep in her heart Simon is always with her and continues to be a guiding presence in her life.

Chapter 38

Oliver

Recurring bad dreams shook Brenda to the core. Time after time, confusing images of her dog dying disrupted her sleep. None of it made any sense at the time but a few years later, a standard poodle named Oliver Twist would connect the dots to this mystery.

Oliver was an eight-week-old energetic ball of white fluff. Brenda quickly realized he was nothing like the calm and adventurous dog she had hoped for when she and her husband decided to get a new puppy.

They lived near the water, went boating and kayaking and wanted to bring Oliver along on all their outdoor adventures.

Oliver wanted nothing to do with any of that. He hated the boat and did not want to go near it. He was highly reactive and had explosive uncontrollable energy.

Oliver grew into a giant, rambunctious comedian. He was also a pickpocket and thief. He once stole a boy's wallet and removed a twenty-dollar bill. He was happiest when he broke the rules, but despite the chaos, Brenda had an incredible bond with him.

One day, Oliver lost his balance and seemed disoriented. They rushed him to the veterinary clinic for a checkup. The doctor started Oliver on antibiotics because of the redness in his ear.

Within a short time, Oliver's condition deteriorated. He had vertigo and could not keep his balance. Tests confirmed Oliver was dying of brain cancer. He had just turned three.

Brenda and her husband faced the shocking reality with dread and watched helplessly as Oliver laid down in his favorite spot by the window. Within minutes he left peacefully cradled in Brenda's arms.

The loss of Oliver sent Brenda into shock as she tried to make sense of it all. She questioned her veterinarian and repeatedly ran every scenario through her mind. She pleaded with her departed mom to greet Oliver. For nine days she barely moved.

On the tenth day, she got out of bed.

An unseen force commanded Brenda to paint a picture of Oliver. Brenda's mom was an artist. Perhaps she was guiding her during this tragic time.

Almost without thinking about it, the painting was done, and the deep pain lifted. The whimsical paisley design on Brenda's easel reflected Oliver's playful free-spirited charm. She posted the artwork on social media, and it went viral. Orders began to pour in.

The animals Brenda painted began to speak to her through their photos and their unique personalities emerged. Intrigued by their messages, Brenda researched the afterlife and past lives when suddenly a light bulb went off. She realized that Oliver had been in multiple past lives with her. That explained their uncanny connection and her recurring dreams.

Oliver continues to make his presence known around the house. Brenda's other dog, Josie, often alerts when no one is there. There is little doubt that Oliver is up to his old antics again.

His presence is felt daily, and his whimsical spirit inspires every portrait. Brenda has completed over one hundred and fifty paintings, and orders keep rolling in.

Chapter 39

Blocked Signs

There are many reasons why signs from the afterlife may be blocked. The most common cause is tied to your emotions.

The memories and feelings you hold onto are so painful that every sign I send gets blocked. They bounce back like a ping pong ball.

This is normal and happens quite often.

There are a few steps you can take to speed that process along. When you release the thoughts that no longer serve you, the energy shifts. You will feel lighter and more balanced.

The most crucial step is to avoid negativity. This includes your thoughts about yourself or what happened to me. Avoid people who drain your energy, such as those who complain or gossip all the time or people who do not support your loss.

Make a conscious decision to counteract the negative energy by doing one nice thing for yourself daily. You can also ask someone for help.

It can be something simple such as bringing you a fresh cup of coffee or tea first thing in the morning. Maybe you want them to sit quietly with you or go for a walk.

These acts may seem insignificant, but they add up and, over time, will eventually replace the negative thoughts.

You have the power to take inspired action every day to allow my messages to come through.

Chapter 40

Congo

Congo was an African Grey parrot who lived with his dad, Brandon, for twenty-nine years. He came from an abusive home and was severely neglected. He had been locked in a filthy, cramped cage with two other parrots. He was terrified to be in a cage, so Brandon gave him a large perch with a play area full of toys. It took months to gain his trust, but with much love and patience, he became the brightest part of Brandon's life.

Congo was a great friend and companion, and he adored Brandon. They bonded over music, and Congo would sit on the piano and pluck the keys with his beak. He could also be a troublemaker. In the wee hours of the morning, he woke Brandon up by mimicking the sound of a frog. It was not the sound of a cute little frog. It was the sound of a giant bullfrog croaking.

Congo disliked it when Brandon slept in on weekends, so he would sneak into his room and rifle through his underwear drawer, flinging countless pairs of boxer briefs on the floor. He also hid the car keys when Brandon was showering so he could not go to work.

When Congo did not get his favorite pistachio treats, he knocked books off tables, pulled picture frames off the walls, and removed the laces from Brandon's shoes. One night, after Brandon worked late, he found that Congo had nearly chewed the legs off the piano. Brandon loved him so much none of his mischievous behavior bothered him. He loved his feathered friend like no other.

After Congo died unexpectedly from a cancerous tumor, Brandon shut down emotionally. He stopped playing the piano, refused offers from friends to socialize, and sat in silence for days on end.

Brandon's mom Christine was worried about her son. She stopped by one day to check on him and brought several books about the afterlife. She tried gently to convince him that Congo was alive and well in another dimension, but Brandon was not interested in all that *woo-woo hocus-pocus nonsense.* The books sat untouched on the coffee table for months collecting dust.

Brandon was on the front porch late one night, staring at the sky. In an emotional outburst, he screamed out loud, yelling at Congo.

"Why did you have to die?" Brandon asked. "I miss you so much. I need to know you are okay." His voice trailed off into uncontrollable sobs.

Months of pent-up sorrow and anger spewed forth. With his head in his hands, Brandon wept like he had not done since he was a little boy.

As he sat alone in misery, he started talking to Congo. Brandon soon realized he had never told Congo he loved him. He hated himself for that. *What a jerk I am,* he thought.

Congo *was my world, my everything, and I never told him how much I loved him.* Brandon had never loved anyone as much as he loved him. This was a different kind of love. It was a kindred spirit kind of love.

Brandon desperately cried out, "Congo, I love you so much. I am so sorry I never told you that. I miss you, buddy. Please, forgive me."

Suddenly, Brandon heard a loud thud from inside the house. He got up to see what made the noise. He looked around but could not find anything out of place. Then he noticed something on the floor next to the coffee table.

The books from his mom were spread out on display. A wave of goosebumps washed over Brandon. He stared at the books, realizing nothing could have knocked them off the coffee table. Nothing except Congo. He picked up the books and began reading.

That was the beginning of a tidal wave of signs from Congo. The more Brandon read about the afterlife, the more his mind opened. He felt lighter than he had in months. He slowly realized that Congo's energy was alive in another dimension, and he could still connect with him. Nothing could keep them apart.

Night after night, he devoured each chapter. He read how to send messages with great interest and practiced sending love to Congo. Brandon pictured big Valentine-shaped hearts with the words, *I Love You,* inside. He never told anyone what he was doing. Not even his mom. He kept this between him and his buddy.

One morning, Brandon was making breakfast and a thought popped into his mind. He knew Congo loved to imitate a bullfrog, so he asked him to send a frog as a sign he was near. He closed his eyes and relaxed. It took several attempts, but soon Brandon thought he saw the vague outline of a grayish-white frog in his mind. He thought it was wishful thinking, so he tried again and said, "Congo, if it is really you, make the frog green."

Nothing happened. He tried again and focused hard, asking for a green frog. Still nothing. No frogs, no shapes, nothing. Brandon's hopes sank. *Just as I thought, he said to himself, this is all a bunch of hocus-pocus nonsense.*

The next day, Brandon was at lunch with a coworker. They were sitting on the outdoor patio enjoying the warm weather. As they talked about an upcoming presentation, Brandon noticed movement from the corner of his eye. He looked to his right, and on the wall next to him was a little green frog. *No way,* he thought. That was just a coincidence. Brandon and his coworker watched in awe as the frog moved closer and seemed to stare at him.

"I think he likes you," his coworker said jokingly. "Those are eyes of love."

They finished lunch under the little green frog's gaze and returned to work. Brandon could not stop thinking about what happened. He began to wonder if maybe it was a sign from Congo. Maybe all that afterlife stuff was real. He would soon discover that was just the tip of the afterlife iceberg.

Brandon began to hear frogs wherever he went, even inside buildings and elevators. Frogs also started to appear everywhere. His mom dropped off a little stuffed green frog holding balloons for his birthday. He brushed it off as a coincidence although he never told anyone about how he asked Congo for that sign. But the frogs kept appearing. It reminded him of an episode of *The Twilight Zone* he had watched as a kid. Millions of frogs invaded, taking over everything. He chuckled at the thought.

The final convincing sign appeared when he came home from work one day and was opening his mail. He glanced at a pair of shoes by the door and noticed the laces had been pulled out. He had just worn them the day before, and they were laced up as usual. Brandon's heart soared.

Once he released all the emotions he had held onto for so long, he made room for signs and messages to appear. In the early hours of the morning, he can hear a bullfrog croaking ever so softly. It brings so much comfort to know Congo is still there.

Brandon found peace and opened his heart to a new African Grey parrot. Tiki was rescued from a neglectful and abusive home. She was terrified of everything for the first few months, but they slowly built a strong connection.

Brandon knows Congo approves of Tiki and has already started influencing her. She began making frog noises without any prompting and loves plucking the piano keys. But the most significant sign was when Brandon woke up one morning and found his boxer briefs scattered all over the floor.

There are no set timelines for healing or opening to signs. If you are sensitive, it may take longer to release those deep emotions. Those feelings are often buried as they are too painful to deal with.

There is no wrong or right way to manage how or when you release what no longer serves you. Some people will hold onto it forever. Maybe you are holding on because you think letting go of those painful memories means letting go of me. It may seem like the last bit of me that you still have but I promise, it is not. There is so much more ahead.

Chapter 41

No Signs

There is a possibility that you may not receive any signs or messages. If you are in this category, you may feel defeated.

With all the hundreds of ways I can send a sign, you are probably wondering why you have not received anything that even closely resembles an afterlife message.

Let me explain.

First, it may be just my personality.

If I was quiet and reserved, I would have those same qualities in the afterlife.

My signs may be so subtle you cannot sense them.

Next, if I spend most of my time within your space and energy, you may not be able to notice any signs. When we share the same energy, you become desensitized to my presence.

I may not feel the need to send anything else because I am with you, and that is all I need. I am filled with so much love, am whole, and have no needs.

It is also essential that you remember that this is my afterlife journey. What I do may or may not be what you want, but it is the highest and best good for my soul.

Someday, when you get to the afterlife, you can decide if you will send signs and messages. You may not feel the need to do so. You will understand that it does not reflect the lack of love if you do not send them. It is just personal preference.

Finally, there is a very good chance that you have received signs and messages, but you did not notice.

Life can be hectic. You are bombarded daily with noise, electronics, media, family, and careers. There are many demands upon you, and they do an excellent job of blocking my messages.

Embracing your experience and using that momentum to move forward and take inspired action is the key.

Chapter 42

Name Signs

My name will always be precious to me. It is embedded in every moment we share. I know how much it means to you, as it means the world to me — especially nicknames.

When my name appears on a sign, license plate, billboard, game, or in a book, know I am near. You were meant to be in that place at that exact moment.

You will feel a tug in your heart and sense something special that just happened. My name resonates with our energy and seeing it or hearing it takes your breath away.

Time will stand still, and you may feel the warmth of my love wash over you. I will find creative ways to send my name as a sign when you least expect it or when your mind is distracted.

Chapter 43

Coco

Coco was Donna's nineteen-year-old blue-eyed Siamese cat with the typical markings of the breed, a black mask on her face, legs, and tail, and a cream-colored body.

Coco was a sweet, affectionate cat who loved playing fetch with a rolled-up facial tissue. As the years passed, Donna and Coco formed a close bond. However, their idyllic life ended when Donna became involved with an abusive, controlling man.

To escape his torment, Donna became addicted to prescription painkillers and spent most of her days in a fog. The painkillers were the only escape from his abuse.

It was a dark time for Donna. Unable to function, she withdrew into isolation. She was grateful for Coco as her love was the one thing Donna always counted on.

As her relationship with her abuser deteriorated, Coco's behavior drastically changed. Once so loving and affectionate, Coco avoided Donna and became distant.

Donna brushed off the odd behavior as a sign of aging. But one night, her world came crashing down.

Donna was in the living room, and Coco was in the kitchen with that man. Suddenly Coco bolted toward Donna and had a massive seizure and died.

Donna was shocked and had no idea what had happened in the kitchen or what caused the seizure. Nothing made any sense.

She had lost the one and only companion who truly loved her. The pain was unbearable, and Donna slipped further into a dark depression.

Subjected to constant emotional abuse, Donna had been beaten down on every level. She knew she had to break free. In a final desperate attempt to escape her abuser, Donna found the strength to leave.

Donna worked hard on her journey into sobriety and created a better life for herself. It was a slow and tedious process, but she moved forward and felt better.

Everything was looking up when a random conversation with a family friend brought devastation upon her again.

Donna learned that her abuser bragged to a family friend about how he physically tormented Coco. The extent of the atrocities of abuse he inflicted upon an innocent cat cannot be revealed, but it was deplorable.

His evil, obsessive behavior was left unchecked as Donna was unaware of what he was doing to her beloved Coco. In shocking detail, Donna learned about the years of torment Coco silently endured. Donna finally understood why Coco's behavior drastically changed.

Donna felt guilty for not protecting her sweet kitty. Her addiction left her emotionally absent in the last three years of Coco's life. Her abuser must have done something to Coco in the kitchen the night she died.

It all started to make sense. Horrific images were embedded in Donna's mind in a never-ending loop.

Unable to forgive herself or her abuser for what happened to Coco, she turned to her friend Jane for moral support. Jane shared similar beliefs in spirituality and topics such as the afterlife.

Once Donna understood the laws of attraction and how holding negative thoughts brings more negativity, she consciously decided to change her beliefs to heal.

Donna practiced acceptance and positive thoughts. Suddenly, she began to receive a multitude of signs from Coco.

Ladybugs appeared everywhere and Donna found a feather in her dresser drawer. Donna did not have birds or down comforters in her home. The feather seemed to be placed where she would see it. Beautiful butterflies fluttered and hovered around her for unusually long periods.

Clouds appeared in the shape of Coco, and lights flickered. Donna was at home alone one day when she heard a cat racing through the house. It was so loud she heard the claws ripping into the carpet. When she got up to investigate, she found her other cats asleep in a different room.

Donna also received a message on her birthday. She was in a gift shop when the resident cat came strolling up to her. The shop's owner said, "Oh, that's our Coco saying hello."

Donna accepted that she never set out to harm Coco or place her in harm's way. They endured insurmountable pain and, more importantly, tremendous courage.

Donna committed to be positive and no longer allows negativity to surround Coco's memory. She focuses on self-forgiveness and remembers all the blessings from Coco.

Donna has been sober for over sixteen years. She has conquered addiction and has risen above the horrors of the past.

The floodgates have opened, and the messages keep pouring in. Donna hears and sees Coco's name almost everywhere she goes.

With Coco by her side, Donna has found the strength to create the beautiful and balanced life she deserves.

Chapter 44

Songs and Musical Signs

Pay close attention when you hear a song on the radio and your heart skips a beat or tears flow.

Songs and musical signs hold many different layers of messages.

The lyrics may have a specific meaning, or the melody may evoke a happy memory from our past.

Songs may also reflect current situations in your life just to let you know I see what you are going through, and you are not alone.

The lyrics may answer questions or guide you during difficult times.

I also may repeatedly send you our favorite song to let you know I am near.

Songs activate the creative part of your brain. This raises your vibration and amplifies my presence.

Musical messages connect you to higher realms and other dimensions, such as the afterlife. When a song makes you think about me, I am surrounded by waves of love.

Even if there are a few tears, the love behind those tears matters most. When you receive a musical sign, turn the volume up and sing along.

Chapter 45

Warning Signs

In the days leading up to my last breath, there may or may not have been warning signs that my time was ending.

Even if you knew how much time I had left, it is unlikely you would have been able to prepare yourself for my departure.

No one wants to think about those things. It is normal to push those thoughts out of your mind and disregard the warning signs.

Regardless of what caused my life to end, remember how masterful animals are at covering up underlying health issues.

In the animal kingdom, illness and injury are signs of weakness. This survival tactic evolved millions of years ago and has nothing to do with your judgment.

Even if you think you missed something, you are not to blame.

Mother Nature is a powerful force, so when you do not realize something is wrong, you haven't failed me. Accidents or other unexpected injuries are no different.

Sometimes, events are beyond your control. I never think about an accident as being your fault.

It is devastating when you miss the warning signs. Perhaps you hoped that whatever it was would pass and I would improve.

Maybe you got busy and skipped my medications or disregarded my fading appetite. Perhaps you noticed I was not sleeping in my normal spot, or I just was not myself.

It all seemed so insignificant at the time.

It is easy to blame yourself.

You may feel that you missed obvious warning signs but there is usually more to the story than you realize.

There could have been a different outcome had you made another decision, but chances are that something else would have transpired that would have ended my life.

When our time on Earth is over, there is little anyone can do to alter that outcome. We all have exit points in our lifetime.

They are like off-ramps on the highway. If you miss your exit, there will be one just down the road.

Some things are meant to be.

Hopefully, you will find it in your heart to let that part of our story go. After all, good things can emerge from every experience. There is even a positive side to grief.

Let me explain...

Chapter 46

Good Grief

Not all grief is bad.

Grief can be good.

I know that sounds crazy because when you are in pain, there is nothing good about it.

From my perspective, when you grieve, you react to losing me. That means that you loved me so much that not having me there in physical form hurts you deeply.

Your grief also reflects our deep bonds of love and all the adventures we shared. So, for me, that is a good thing.

That means I meant the world to you and that I am special.

That makes me feel good.

I do not want to see you in pain, but avoiding loss is impossible.

You lost someone you love dearly.

Allow yourself time to grieve.

Experiencing grief means you are going through a physical, emotional, and spiritual shift.

This can be good for you.

Most humans do not grow spiritually when life is easy — growth results when something catastrophic or tragic launches you out of your comfort zone.

Losing me would qualify as both of those.

You may begin to seek answers, gain a greater understanding, or question everything when something disruptive happens.

Remember, grieving is okay, and I wish they would teach this to kids in school.

Most people do not have good experiences to draw from after they suffer a loss.

Many feel alienated and unable to cope.

I believe this goes back to childhood.

Maybe your parents said things like, *stop crying, or I'll give you something to cry about.*

Or perhaps they said, *it was just a goldfish. I will get you another one.*

Sadly, many parents mean well, but they do not always know how to comfort a child, and their words make the loss even worse.

Many children become confused and withdraw when they suffer a loss, which is how they react as an adult. They simply do not know how else to react.

Grief reflects the love you share with someone no longer with you. Therefore, the more deeply you love, the more deeply you grieve.

If you are in that deep level of grief, you have been blessed to have someone so spectacular and exceptional in your life that it caused significant pain and emotional trauma when you lost them.

Many never feel that beautiful connection or that intense closeness with anyone else.

Why is grief good for you?

You are here in this lifetime to experience everything possible: the ups and downs, the good and the bad.

The more experiences you have, the more evolved your soul becomes.

The more evolved your soul becomes, the easier you and I can communicate and stay connected even from different dimensions.

Your energetic fingerprint or vibration naturally increases when you have moved through grief into healing. It is like a car wash for your soul.

When you activate healing, you sparkle, shine, and glow with a brilliant new light.

When a shift happens,

a domino effect of energy is set into motion.

That transformation is powerful.

You shifted your thoughts and expressed gratitude for the time we spent together.

You opened your mind to new perspectives, searched for answers, found acceptance, and grew in body, mind, and spirit.

That is *good grief.*

When this shift happens, it creates a domino effect of activity in your energy field. You start building your future by leaving the past and all those painful thoughts behind. You become the creator of your new life.

Anything can happen, and the possibilities are limitless.

Think about that for a moment.

How amazing is that?

As you can see, there is a good side to grief.

It is not fun to endure, and I have yet to meet anyone who enjoys it, but hopefully, you can see the bigger picture.

Stay in the moment and feel all that comes your way. It is okay to grieve. You are in control of the mighty ship called *grief.*

You decide when to set sail, when to bank starboard, and when to drop anchor.

It may not feel like it, but you control that vessel.

Like on a real ship, there is a starting point and a final destination.

So, when you set sail, keep your eyes ahead on the horizon.

If you focus only on the past, you will run aground.

At the very least, it will take you much longer to arrive at your healing port, and supplies will likely run out.

Be patient with yourself and those around you.

It is in those moments when a shift occurs. You have my permission to smile again.

You were the first to love me and the last to hold me.

Your heart can love again.

Once you grasp this, I can manifest as your copilot.

You do not want to miss that.

After all, we have exciting adventures that await us, and I cannot think of anyone I would rather be with than you.

Now, it is time for me to hand the baton over to Karen.

She will share actual messages from the afterlife sessions she conducted.

There will also be insight into reincarnation and how to raise your vibration to receive more signs and so much more.

In the following story, one very lucky dog finds a way to get an unexpected message to help his grieving mom.

Chapter 47

LuckyDuck

The silence in Beth's apartment was too much to bear.

Both of her parents died several years ago, and their beloved dog, Tessie, who came to live with her, recently passed away. Beth felt so alone.

One night, she couldn't sleep, so she opened her laptop. She randomly navigated to her social media profile.

The first post in the news feed caught her eye.

There was a little brown puppy with a broken leg.

Beth clicked on the post to read more.

The puppy was likely thrown from a moving vehicle to sustain so many severe injuries. They were trying to raise funds for his surgery as no one had claimed him.

Donations were coming in slowly and not nearly enough to reach their goal. The puppy would be euthanized the next day if the clinic did not receive enough money to cover the surgery.

He was only about twelve pounds, with long brown fur, a white chest, and a large plume of a tail. They guessed he was a dachshund, Papillion, or sheltie mix.

Something about his eyes captured Beth's heart.

Beth donated the remaining lump sum for the puppy's much-needed surgery in an act of kindness that activated what can only be described as *destiny*.

After a few weeks, Beth checked in with the clinic and found out the puppy's leg had been amputated.

Thanks to Beth, the lucky pup got the surgery he needed. He was recovering in a foster home near her.

One day, Beth was going to a friend's house and stopped at a pet warehouse to buy treats for her friend's dogs.

There was an adoption event that day, but it was not until she was in line to check out that she noticed a small brown puppy in a crate.

Beth asked if the puppy was sick, and the store clerk told her he wasn't ready to adopt. He needed post-operative care from a leg amputation.

Beth peered inside the crate.

Those eyes. She recognized his eyes.

This can't be, she thought to herself. *Is this the exact puppy I donated to? What are the chances of that?*

The Universe has a way of bringing us together at precisely the right time, and this was one of those moments.

Beth's heart jumped, and she quickly met with the rescuer to find out more. They immediately recognized her as the kindhearted soul who made the large donation that saved this puppy's life.

Beth never went to her friend's house because she spent the rest of the day next to the little brown puppy with the cone around his neck. She instantly fell in love with him.

The rescue facility needed someone to care for him for a few days. Beth joyfully agreed and took the puppy and a bag of new toys home.

The first few days with this injured pup were not exactly a fairytale. The clinic named him Lucky, and he was barely a year old. Lucky did not take long to show Beth he was severely traumatized. Once she was home and got him settled, she reached out to pet him, and he lashed out in fear and bit her.

Lucky was insecure, and he did not trust her. Beth needed to slow down and ease into this. Message received loud and clear.

Beth had never had an aggressive dog and was not quite sure how to handle a snarling ball of fluff. Any attempt she made to pet him, feed him or be near him ended up with bloodshed and bandages.

One time she ended up in the hospital with a severe bite. Anyone else would have taken this puppy back and wiped their hands clean of him — anyone except Beth.

After several weeks passed, Beth signed the adoption papers and changed his name to LuckyDuck.

They carved out their new life for the next eight years, and Beth kept the house stocked with antiseptic and bandages.

Although some of LuckyDuck's emotional scars never healed, he finally accepted her affection, although total strangers were still fair game as were her friends.

They learned quickly not to pet the cute fluffy puppy.

One day, Beth was petting LuckyDuck's belly and discovered a large mass. She brought him to the clinic for an exam.

The vet confirmed it was a cancerous testicle. LuckyDuck was neutered before she adopted him, but this testicle never descended, so it was never removed.

The doctor recommended surgery right away.

Beth did her best to stay positive, but she was anxious and worried.

After his surgery, LuckyDuck healed well, but Beth kept close watch over him. The two of them were at home relaxing when a song called *Peter Gunn* played on the jazz station.

Beth happened to notice LuckyDuck's face when the song played. He had a look that said, *pay attention; this song is important.*

She made a mental note of the song, wondering why this of all songs would be important.

Beth's worst fears became a reality when she found another lump on LuckyDuck's abdomen a few months later. The doctor said the cancer was back, and it was growing fast. Beth scheduled the surgery and prayed for positive news.

When he made it out of surgery, Beth was so relieved, but later that night, the doctor called and said LuckyDuck's condition was declining.

Beth's heart dropped out of her chest. She flew out the door, but by the time she arrived at the clinic, LuckyDuck was gone. He was only nine years old. Beth's world went blank.

The waves of guilt hit immediately. She questioned whether she made the right decisions, and grief took over her life. The emptiness from the loss of her boy was too much to bear.

Beth found some comfort in reading a few books on the afterlife, including mine. The stories helped her endure the pain, especially during the holiday season.

Intrigued with animal communication, Beth joined my practice group on Facebook. She was surprised to see Frank in the group. She read about his reincarnation story with Captain, and it was one of her favorites.

Beth followed the steps to connect, hoping to get a message from LuckyDuck, but nothing happened.

Determined to communicate with her boy, she started each day with gratitude and asked LuckyDuck to send specific signs.

She requested hummingbirds and the song *Peter Gunn*. She also asked for his name to appear. The next day, Beth got a huge surprise.

I was in my office preparing for my day with a morning meditation and blessing.

I asked silently if anyone in the spirit realm had a message to share.

Within seconds, a little fluffy brown dog appeared.

I recognized him from Beth's pictures. Those eyes, that face, his fur. It was LuckyDuck.

An immense wave of love washed over me.

Tell Mom I am always near. I love it when she says my name.

So much gratitude was coming through. I felt his love for Beth.

I asked him if he had anything else he wanted to share.

LuckyDuck showed me something blue and an angel. I was not sure what it meant but hoped Beth would understand.

I wrote down his brief messages, not realizing their monumental significance, and planned to share them with Beth once I started up my computer.

I sent his energy back and thanked him for the messages.

I emailed his messages to Beth and she quickly replied.

Beth had not slept well the night before and was on the lanai that morning trying to connect with LuckyDuck. She turned her phone off so she could concentrate.

She meditated for a while, opened her heart to LuckyDuck, and anxiously waited for a message.

She asked for a sign, a message, anything to show he was near.

Nothing came through. She didn't feel, see, or hear anything. Discouraged, she blamed herself for not being able to receive his communication. She turned her phone back on and heard a ping.

It was my email.

Beth was shocked when she read the messages from LuckyDuck. She immediately understood what he meant by something blue and the angel reference. Her heart skipped a beat as she responded to my message. Her fingers were typing as fast as she could. Emotions welled up in her heart.

This was incredible!

I read Beth's response in total awe.

Above her bed was a wind chime with a little dog on top with *blue wings.*

There was also a bear with *angel wings* holding a *blue star* that said, *When in doubt...Look up.*

Next to her bed, on the side table, were several *blue stones and blue crystals.*

On the wall above the crystals was a photo collage of LuckyDuck.

The final moment of proof came when Beth shared the significance of the date I received the messages.

It was the anniversary of LuckyDuck's transition.

That morning Beth's journey through grief turned a corner.

That short message broke through the dense fog of pain which gripped her for so long.

Healing was activated, and the heaviness upon her heart began to lift.

That simple message was life-changing and precisely what Beth had been praying for.

Afterlife signs from LuckyDuck continue to come through.

The words *lucky* and *duck* frequently appear wherever she goes, and the song *Peter Gunn* plays on her devices in mysterious ways without prompting.

Beth is sure LuckyDuck showed her how to be brave in the face of adversity and taught her to live her life to the fullest.

She has no doubt he had something to do with bringing her new puppy, Lakota, into her life.

She is forever changed after losing her soulmate, LuckyDuck, but now the grief does not hold a candle to the amount of joy and tremendous gratitude in her heart.

Chapter 48

Afterlife Sessions

Every session I conducted was unique, and I never knew what the animals would say or who they would bring through.

Despite their differences, I noticed some common themes and patterns emerge, bringing incredible insight into our world and beyond.

Primarily, what we think our animal companions experience when they transition is often completely different.

Their perspectives highlight what was truly important to them and not necessarily what we obsess about.

For instance, if a client wanted details about their beloved companion's tragic or painful ending, the animals would likely avoid that subject and move on to something more positive.

Interestingly, the animals almost always focus on love or happy memories and not on their final moments.

Very few shared any details about the things we lose sleep over.

This underlying theme was pivotal in my life too.

These heartfelt messages changed the way I managed myself with each loss I endured.

When I interviewed each client for this book, I was deeply moved by the profound healing most of them shared and delighted to hear them describe the meanings behind the messages I am about to share.

I never fully understood how impactful and life-changing their experiences were until now.

What happened after their appointments was remarkable, as you will soon discover.

Here are their stories.

Chapter 49
Holly and Angus

Toni was skeptical and unsure of what to expect when she scheduled her first session with me. Her goal was to find out how to provide better care for Holly, her fourteen-year-old red sable German shepherd.

Holly would be instrumental in opening her heart and mind to animal communication through our sessions. Her messages would later give Toni the strength she needed when it was time to say goodbye.

I admired Holly's photograph and her unique reddish-brown coat as I began the session. I invited her energy to join us and sharpened my focus.

A tidal wave of love washed over me when I told Holly how gorgeous she was. I sensed her strong bond with her family, and the messages started to flow.

"Her energy is coming through loud and clear," I said, "Holly wants you to know she is *perfect*."

I had no idea how important that message was then, and Toni missed it too. She was so focused on absorbing everything that was happening she didn't catch it either. Her husband, Mike, picked up on the meaning of the word *perfect* as he listened to the recording the next day. He reminded Toni that she constantly told Holly that she was *Mommy's perfect girl* and *Mommy's perfect princess*.

Perfect, she was. Born on December 16th, Holly was named for the holiday season, and Toni and Mike quickly fell in love with her after they brought the eight-week-old puppy home. She was gentle and sweet, and everyone was her friend. She went to work with Toni every day at her flower shop.

"What is going on with her toes?" I asked. "She keeps showing me her toes."

Toni shared that Holly had severe arthritis that calcified in the joints of her feet, and her toes were inflamed, causing discomfort and stiffness when she walked. Toni was shocked that I would know about Holly's toes, as she had not provided any details about Holly's health issues.

"Holly also wants me to talk about *your toes*, Toni," I said, "What is going on with *your toes*?"

There was silence on the other end of the phone.

"I have an ongoing issue with my toe that required multiple surgeries," Toni said slowly.

How could Karen possibly know about my toe? Toni thought to herself.

"Holly also shows me a rupture and something breaking apart," I said. "Do you know what she is referring to?"

"Holly has three ruptured discs in the lumbar region of her spine, and a section had calcified," Toni said, "Somehow, that section cracked and broke apart, causing ongoing mobility issues."

Toni and I were both amazed at how detailed Holly's message was. This was not hip dysplasia or other commonly known medical issues for a German shepherd. This was a unique condition and specific to Holly.

As I refocused, more messages streamed in.

"Holly keeps showing me the letter *A*," I said, "Do you know what this means?"

"That is our Chihuahua, Angus," Toni said, "Holly adores him."

Many other messages came through, but the final message from Holly was pivotal in preparing Toni for the day that she knew was coming.

"Does she still want to be here?" Toni asked.

"This is very hard for me to share, Toni, but Holly is very clear about this. She will never be able to answer that question. Her desire to protect and stay with you is too strong," I said, "She won't give any indications that she is ready to go, not a look, nothing. You will have to make that decision yourself someday."

After that session, Toni and Mike decided they would not waste another precious moment they had left and celebrated every day. They showered Holly with special treats like pupa-chinos, a creamy frozen dog dessert. They took an insane number of photographs, provided her with high-quality meals, and treated her like royalty. They focused only on positive thoughts, happy energy, and living life with Holly to the fullest.

They realized it was wasteful to focus on the negative aspect of Holly's health issues or obsess about how long she would be with them. They wanted to honor their perfect girl every single day.

About three months later, the day finally arrived that Toni and Mike had been dreading. Holly was having more and more difficulty with her mobility, and they realized it was her time to go.

They had done their best and given her everything they could, but Holly was now over fifteen years old. Just as Holly shared in the session, she never once gave them any indication that she was ready to leave, and ultimately, they had to make that fateful decision themselves. Surrounded by her loving family, Holly took her last breath.

It wasn't long before they started noticing the afterlife signs from Holly. Toni found pennies wherever she went. Mike was playing a video game and earned enough points for a virtual dog. The computer randomly picked the name *Holly* to be his dog.

On two different occasions, Mike let his arm hang off the bed where Holly used to sleep, and he felt the warmth of her body under his hand. When he looked, nothing was there, but he was sure it was her.

Another time, Holly was clearly in the room with Toni when she felt the mattress move just as it would when Holly would prop her chin on it. Something pushed down on the mattress, but there was no one there.

About a year after Holly transitioned, Toni had an intensely vivid dream where she and Holly were face to face. It was so real, and Toni could feel her fur as she held her. Holly was so happy and kept saying, *I'm perfect, I'm beautiful just as you remember,* and *I'm checking on you.* Toni could feel how much Holly loved them. In that dream, Holly said she had the best life and everything she needed. Toni woke up smiling with tears of happiness in her eyes.

Everything shifted when the holidays arrived. All the memories of their last fifteen years together rushed into Toni's mind. Besides the raw pain, she felt empty inside and did not want to decorate or celebrate the season. It was like losing Holly all over again.

One day, Toni was in her car going to work when the radio announced that the next song would be, *A Holly Jolly Christmas*. Toni felt a stabbing pain inside her chest as that was the song they sang to Holly all the time, not just during the holidays. Holly would cock her head to the side each time she heard her name. It was too much for Toni to bear, so she turned the radio off.

Later that day, she was driving home, and once again, that song came on the radio. Unable to cope, Toni turned it off. She could not bear to hear that song. She drove home in silence. She opened the door and that same song played on the radio.

"Mike, you won't believe this. I heard the *Holly Jolly* song come on twice on the way home, and twice I turned it off," Toni said, "I'm just not ready to hear it."

"Let it play," Mike said, "Holly is here and wants us to hear it. *Just let it play.*"

Toni finally relented, and they listened to the song together and reminisced about their perfect girl.

After Christmas, Mike deleted all the holiday music from their playlist, but every so often, without any logical explanation, that *Holly Jolly Christmas* song plays by itself.

Angus

Toni scheduled another phone session after Holly transitioned to check in with Angus, their black and tan apple head Chihuahua. Losing Holly was hard on Angus too, and he mourned her loss. She also wanted to hear from Holly and see how she was doing in the afterlife.

I connected with little Angus and felt his energy come swirling through.

"Angus is such a stoic little fellow," I said.

"Everyone describes him that way," Toni answered, "He never complains and is so content just to be near us."

"He says the word, RANCH, or BRANCH. I am not quite sure which one. Some words sound the same as they come in so quickly." I said, "Do you understand this?"

"Yes!" Toni said, "Right outside my window is the dogwood tree we planted in honor of Holly. Angus can see the branches through the window."

"Okay," I said, "He is so excited to talk about a curling ribbon. Does that make any sense?"

Toni looked around the room and said, "Yes! I got a birthday balloon a few weeks ago, and it is tied to the back of the chair with a curling ribbon."

"I can feel how deeply he misses Holly," I said, "So I am showing him how to connect with her energy. Now he will always know she is near."

I shifted my focus to Holly. She came through as beautiful and *perfect* as ever. She shared her love and devotion to her family.

"Holly shows me a box with her name on it and says it is in the room with you. Do you know what she is referring to?" I asked.

"I do! We are mailing some of Holly's remains to a company that makes memorial artwork out of blown glass." Toni said, "Her ashes will be added to the glass. I have that box sitting right here with her name on it."

There was a sense of peace when the session ended. Toni felt much lighter and relieved to hear Holly was alive and well in spirit.

When the day came to say goodbye to Angus, Toni and Mike were devastated but knew from their past sessions that Holly would be there to greet him.

After his transition, they often sensed Angus in his favorite spots around the house, which brought great comfort. Toni felt him next to her ankle, and Mike saw him sitting on his blanket on the sofa. It was just a flash but undeniably Angus.

Further confirmation came one night when Toni had the most vivid dream. Holly and Angus were together and looked so happy. Then with a smile, Holly said they were both *perfect*.

Chapter 50

Shady

Linda scheduled a session to connect with her recently departed fourteen-year-old cat, Shady.

Losing him deeply affected her; she needed to know he was okay in the afterlife.

Shady was a young stray cat with medium-length gray fur, white whiskers, and yellow eyes. He showed up in their yard one day many years ago and never left. He loved to play fetch with her kids and was unphased by all their rambunctious activity.

The kids called him Shady because he liked to spend time in the shady area under the trees. Shady was lovable and silly and soon stole everyone's heart.

I opened the session with Shady and felt a waterfall of loving emotions wash over me. His energy was light and balanced, and he was eager to share his messages. I described his energy as Linda listened quietly.

Shady quickly showed me an image of white mice. They were everywhere. He did not share any more information despite my asking.

I was unsure if he was showing me a toy or, perhaps, a bigger problem, such as an infestation. I carefully chose my words.

"I am not quite sure how to say this, Linda," I said, "Please don't be offended, but Shady says I need to talk about white mice. He does not share any other details, so do you know what this is? Is there a mouse or rodent problem? He insists I talk about them."

"No, I don't have a rodent problem," Linda said slowly. "I have no idea what that is about."

Suddenly, she remembered what was in her hand.

Before her appointment, Linda made sure she had Shady's favorite toy.

He loved his little white furry mice. He chased them all over the house, and she would find them everywhere.

"Oh my gosh, Karen, I can't believe this," Linda said. "I have Shady's white mice in my hand. He loved to play with them, and I forgot I had them. I was so caught up in what you were saying I didn't realize I was holding them!"

Linda took a moment to regain her composure.

Before she called for her appointment, she asked Shady to mention the mice because she still had some doubts that I would actually be communicating with him. This was her way of making sure it was truly Shady.

Once I mentioned the mice, I felt the energy shift. Linda relaxed, and the grief began to lift.

I was relieved when Linda told me there was not a rodent issue, and we still laugh about that message after all these years.

I refocused on Shady's energy.

"Linda, are you a fan of the television show *Gilligan's Island*, or do you like the spice ginger?" I asked. "Shady keeps telling me to say the word *ginger*. Oh, wait, now he says Ginger is with him."

"Ginger was my father-in-law's dog," Linda said, "She was a little wheaten terrier. She passed away a while ago. Only a few family members know about Ginger."

The message was so unexpected, but it made sense Ginger and Shady would be together. Ginger was part of the family and dearly loved. Shady sent more messages and shared his deep love for everyone in his family.

The whole experience set off a chain reaction, allowing healing to begin.

Shady opened Linda's eyes to the afterlife, and she found comfort in knowing he was in a different realm, not gone forever. He even heard her talking about his white mice.

Linda was so relieved that Shady never mentioned the way his life ended. The memory of his final moments haunted her for so long.

Shady had a long healthy life, but one day he started vomiting. After a check-up, the tests found only dehydration, but he stayed at the clinic overnight for observation. Linda sensed something else was wrong because Shady refused to eat and was not acting normally.

The following day the veterinary office called with devastating news. Shady's condition worsened. Linda's heart sank. He was the love of her life, and she begged for this not to be the end. The doctor confirmed her worst fears. Shady was not going to make it.

It was an icy cold January morning, and the driving conditions were not good. Linda could not let Shady die alone, so she got to the clinic as fast as possible.

It was a terrible sight.

Shady was lying on a table while they were giving him oxygen. He had so many tubes in him. Linda had never been through anything like that. He appeared so fragile she did not want to hurt him by picking him up.

No one told her she could hold him.

It was one of her biggest regrets.

Shady went into cardiac arrest shortly after she arrived and was gone.

The emptiness that followed was immense. Linda had never felt so much pain. She wished she could have held him and comforted him. A few weeks later, she had a vivid dream. She felt Shady's soft fur as she held him in her arms. It was so realistic. Shady said he had to go, and she watched him walk away from her.

Linda found solace and comfort with her other rescued cat, Lily. She was a tabby with medium-length fur covered with black, tan, and grey stripes. She had soft yellow eyes and white whiskers.

Linda gently told Lily to give her an unmistakable message when she was ready to leave. She noticed Lily had typical signs of aging, but recently Lily had been losing weight and staring at the water bowl. Linda was worried and watched her closely.

When Lily refused her favorite treat, buttercream, Linda realized it was the end.

The thought of going through another loss was unbearable. The trauma of losing Shady was still fresh, and Linda suffered from recurring panic attacks from post-traumatic stress disorder.

Linda didn't realize she could hold Shady in his final moments. So, she thought about everything she had learned when Shady died. With her husband and daughter by her side, Linda cradled Lily gently in her arms as they all said goodbye.

Lily was surrounded by love as she took her last breath.

The next day, Linda drove into town with the grim task of planning for Lily's cremation. She was grieving deeply and lost in her sadness as she filled out the paperwork. She wondered if she had done the right thing.

It was an empty and helpless feeling, and she quietly asked Shady for a sign it was Lily's time to go. With all her heart, she hoped she had made the right decision and headed out the door.

She noticed something on the driver's side front tire when she got to her car. Linda took a few steps closer and stopped in her tracks. A long six-inch feather was stuck to the side of the tire. She had no idea how it got there or how it was attached to the outside of the tire.

She stared at the feather in disbelief. It was oddly stuck to the tire.

There were no birds near her car, let alone a bird large enough to leave a six-inch feather. Ordinarily, she would not have thought twice about it, but she remembered she had asked Shady for a sign that it was Lily's time to go.

Only Shady would do something so outrageous and unique. As Linda drove home, a sense of peace washed over her as she thanked Shady for the incredible message.

The next few days were a roller coaster of emotions. Along with the crushing pain, Linda was concerned Lily would not find her way to the afterlife when she transitioned because she suffered from dementia. So, she told Lily to find Shady and send a sign she was okay. Linda could not stop worrying and tried desperately not to think about it.

She was in the kitchen near the table when something caught her eye. Gently floating around Lily's favorite chair was a small white feather about one-quarter of an inch long. Linda could not believe her eyes. They did not have pet birds or feather pillows due to allergies. It was the sign she asked for.

"Thank you, Sweet Pea! You've made it home," Linda said aloud with her heart full of gratitude, "You found Shady. I love you both so much. Thank you for letting me know."

Linda kept the tiny feather as a keepsake and reminder that Lily and Shady were together again.

As the weeks passed, more signs appeared. Linda saw license plates with the letters *L I L Y* on them, and one night when the family played a word game, the dice rolled out the letters *S H A D Y*.

Those moments brought so much joy and laughter into their hearts. Linda knows if she pays attention, she will find more signs. Some are more subtle than others, but she never doubts them.

Linda's heart is peaceful, knowing her two angels are alive and well in the afterlife watching over them and their two new cats, Harry and Beyla.

Chapter 51

Julie

On the way to an appointment, Debbie silently asked her recently departed bunny, Julie, to send a sign.

She scanned the skies looking for bunny-shaped clouds. When a white egret flew over her car, Debbie smiled. It would be just like Julie doing things her way.

Debbie had asked Julie to send bunny-shaped clouds as a sign she was near. Instead, Julie sent birds. Lots of birds.

That same day while driving home, a hawk flew above her. It circled unusually low. A wave of emotions and goosebumps washed over Debbie as the hawk soared above.

Later that same day, two more hawks appeared above her on the way to the post office. She marveled at the synchronicity of seeing all those birds and knew her husband, Pete, would be thrilled. He had asked Julie to send birds.

Julie was a small white bunny with blue eyes. She was intelligent and funny and loved her toys. She was litterbox trained and had free range of the house under supervision.

Although Julie was trained not to chew on cords, she could still get into trouble. Once, she pulled all the toilet paper off the roll and made a giant nest. She was so proud of herself and sat in the center, looking quite content.

Julie was the bright spot in their life with her zoomies and antics, especially performing 360-degree leaps in the air.

One day Debbie noticed something was wrong with one of Julie's eyes. Debbie was relieved when it was just a common parasite, so they began treatment with medication.

Despite their efforts, Julie's eye continued to get worse, and with further testing, they found cancer. The news was shocking, and Debbie was worried because rabbits have sensitive systems, and Julie meant everything to her.

The doctors surgically removed her eye, however, Julie's condition continued to decline. Debbie realized she was slipping away. Debbie held her gently, asked loved ones to greet her, and within a short time, Julie was gone.

Devastated, Debbie and her family gathered outside around 10 pm to bury Julie beside their other bunnies. It had been raining, and the sky was cloudy and dark.

In a blur of tears, Debbie looked at the night sky and saw a bunny-shaped cloud resembling Julie. Suddenly, the sky cleared and turned a deep midnight blue color as if on cue, and the Milky Way appeared above. The planets and stars glimmered above them like diamonds in the sky.

Consumed with grief and barely functioning, Debbie began to wonder if there was an afterlife for animals. Some strange things had been happening since Julie transitioned.

Once, a glowing white orb about the size of a soccer ball appeared in her room. Debbie kept blinking, trying to figure out what it was.

Then she saw another orb with sparkles around it. The orb was so close she could have touched it. She was in awe of this light anomaly and wondered what else it could have been.

There were no other lights or reflections to explain this odd glowing light. In her mind's eye, Debbie kept seeing the image of Julie leaping around in 360-degree circles with flowers around her.

Another time Debbie saw Julie's face appear when she was in bed. Debbie was awake, but her eyes were closed. It was so vivid. Julie looked so real she expected to see her when she opened her eyes.

Debbie searched online, downloaded several books about the afterlife, including mine, and devoured every word.

There were tears of relief as she read about the signs from departed pets.

Debbie realized that Julie was not gone forever and felt she was guiding her to me, so she booked an afterlife session.

Debbie called on the day of her appointment, and I invited Julie to join us. I immediately felt Julie's excitement. A feeling of warmth, love, and utter happiness sprang from her. I sensed the close bond between them.

"Julie tells me she was supposed to leave," I said, "No one could have fixed her."

Debbie breathed a sigh of relief.

"I felt responsible for Julie's life ending so soon," Debbie said, "I second-guessed every decision and felt so guilty."

"Julie was ready to go," I said, "She knows you did your best."

I shifted my focus because Julie said the following message was important.

"Julie tells me you have some of her fur. She says to *be sure to tell Mom because this is important*. Does this make sense?"

"Oh, Karen, I know exactly what that means," Debbie said.

"After Julie passed, I gathered her fur as a keepsake," Debbie said, "No one knew about this."

For the next few moments, time stood still. There was electricity in the air. I saw an older female human spirit appear next to Julie.

"Debbie, there is someone with Julie," I said, "She says an M name, like Mary or Marie. Do you know who this is?"

"Yes!" Debbie said, "That's my Aunt Marie! She loved animals, and I asked her to greet Julie when she passed!"

The messages continued and mentioned many other family members that loved Julie. Then I saw a swimming pool.

"Well, this is interesting," I said, "Julie is showing me a pool and wants me to say the word *angel*. Does this make sense to you?"

"Yes!" Debbie said, "We have a pool, and I always called her my *angel bunny*."

Upon hearing Debbie's words, an image of a twisting DNA marker appeared that I recognized right away. This symbol represented past lives, and every strand was one lifetime.

"Julie shows countless past lives you have shared with her," I said, "You must have a very close bond. The more lifetimes you share, the closer your bond."

"We do," Debbie said, "I love all my animals, but there has always been something special about Julie. I could never put my finger on it, but now it makes sense."

Julie was so accurate she told me what types of vehicles they drove, and her bubbly personality came through loud and clear. Like the clouds parting on the night she transitioned, the pain began to lift away from Debbie's heart.

She continues to explore her intuition by actively participating in my animal communication practice group and courses. When Debbie goes on her walk, she asks for signs and usually receives them.

Birds frequently appear and fly unusually close, and once a roadrunner stopped and looked right at her. When she was in her garden, hummingbirds and butterflies lingered and a dragonfly hovered by her face as if saying *hello*.

Once Debbie moved forward into healing, she realized the importance of their connection.

Julie encouraged her to learn about spirituality and to be more mindful of her surroundings. Debbie is more joyful and lives her life with purpose.

Debbie still misses Julie but knows they will always be connected. She truly believes Julie guided her my way to help her heal.

I believe that too.

There is nothing more powerful than the bonds of love.

Chapter 52

Hans

Hans was a twelve-year-old black and tan Yorkshire terrier. He had soft brown eyes and was the love of Cassie's life. He went everywhere with her and was even part of her wedding ceremony.

Hans struggled with digestive issues for most of his life, and when his health declined, Cassie began to second-guess every decision she made. Concerned, she scheduled a check-up for him and never expected that day to end with a goodbye to her sweet boy.

The doctor confirmed Hans was in liver failure and had a poor prognosis. Cassie and her husband had no other option. They tearfully cradled him, and Cassie quietly asked her recently departed grandmother to greet him.

The pain of losing her beloved grandmother was fresh, and now all those emotions came rushing back as Hans took his last breath.

After Hans transitioned, Cassie shared her loss with her colleagues at work. Dr. Blake, and his office manager, Amy, encouraged her to book a session with me. I had been a patient of Dr. Blake's for sixteen years, and they knew me well and trusted my work. Cassie quickly scheduled an appointment.

Cassie and her sister, Kari, called in for her session. I invited Hans to join us and immediately sensed two energies patiently waiting for me. One was an animal, and the other was an older human female.

"Did you lose a grandmother?" I asked.

"Yes, she just recently passed away," Cassie said.

"There is a grandmother energy here, and she wants you to know she is with Hans," I said, "She says he went from your arms into hers when he transitioned."

That was precisely what Cassie imagined when she said goodbye to Hans. She was overjoyed to hear they were together.

"Did your grandmother have a lot of animals? I see horses."

"Yes!" Cassie said, "She had so many animals! My love for animals is from my grandmother."

I shifted my focus to Hans.

"Hans talks about a name that begins with the letters CH. And a name that begins with an E. Do you understand this? I asked.

"Chad is my husband," Cassie said, "and Emma is one of my daughters."

"Hans says he misses his baby girls," I said.

"He loved my daughters," Cassie said, "He was so good with them."

"I don't know where this fits in, but I see the symbols for money or finances," I said. "Hans has a funny name for your husband. He calls him the *money guru*. Does this make sense to you?"

"My husband is in the accounting industry," Cassie said slowly. "Every morning when he left for work, he would say, *have a good day and save money*. He also called Hans, *H-Money*!"

Many other messages that day brought peace to Cassie's broken heart. When I was closing the session, I heard Cassie's grandmother say, *happy birthday*. That message sent Cassie into orbit. Her birthday was just around the corner, and it would have been her first birthday without her grandmother.

Just minutes after they hung up, Cassie and Kari discussed the messages they had just received when they suddenly heard a familiar sound. It was Hans. He did a pre-bark growl that they both heard. Suddenly, Cassie remembered that something strange happened the night before our session.

Cassie was lying awake in bed when the baby monitor in her daughter's room downstairs kept turning on. Her daughter was sound asleep, and it should only be activated by a noise.

She listened again and heard a knocking sound. Cassie was startled when suddenly her daughter was standing beside her bed.

"Mommy, someone's knocking in my room," Emma said.

A wave of fear ran through Cassie, but she had to go downstairs to ensure no one was there. There were only bedrooms downstairs and no exterior doors. Without a logical reason for the knocking sounds, Cassie crept down the stairs, not knowing what she would find.

She slowly entered each room and looked everywhere someone could hide. She found nothing out of place. She never figured out what the source of the knocking was. Cassie did not get much sleep that night.

The next day Cassie was folding laundry, and her mind began to wander. A thought popped into her mind that maybe that knocking sound could have been Hans. She went downstairs and looked around.

She didn't see anything until she opened the closet door in her daughter's room. On the inside of the door were little dog-like scratch marks. She had never seen them before. They were at the perfect height for Hans.

There was no way Hans could have made those marks because a baby gate blocked the stairs.

Inspired and energized by her experience, Cassie finally released the pain that tormented her. A transformation started that day, and a new sense of peace filled her heart.

Cassie has embraced a new perspective that there is more to life after physical death and no longer dwells on negative thoughts.

While the path into healing was not easy, losing two loved ones around the same time, now she has a whole new outlook on life.

Cassie knows that her grandmother and Hans will always be with her, and every day should be cherished with those you love.

Chapter 53

Chloe the Cat

Bethany was devastated when the doctors discovered Chloe, her thirteen-year-old gray cat, had an inoperable tumor. They were constant companions enduring all of life's challenges together.

As time passed, Bethany sensed their time together was ending and desperately searched for the strength and courage to do what was best for Chloe.

She fought back the tears as she gazed into Chloe's yellow eyes. The moment she had dreaded was upon her. Chloe could no longer continue. Bethany reluctantly scheduled the dreaded appointment with her veterinarian.

Even though she knew nothing else could be done, it felt wrong. Within moments of whispering her final goodbye, Bethany suddenly regretted her decision. A wave of dread washed over her. Chloe was gone.

For weeks, Bethany kept running Chloe's final moments through her mind. The only thing that kept her from total despair was her dog, Domino. Although her family and friends offered support, there were few words to ease her pain.

One night a thought came across Bethany's mind that brought a ray of hope. She conducted angel readings and thought if angels could communicate with us, departed pets could too.

She searched online for pet loss resources and downloaded the audio version of my book. That is when the energy shifted. The uplifting stories gave her so much peace and relief for her decision to say goodbye to Chloe.

She began to see a lot of rainbows and sensed they were signs from Chloe. It warmed her heart each time, and while the pain was still raw, Bethany felt the heaviness of grief begin to lift.

While driving down a busy road one day, Bethany spotted a stray cat that needed help. The black and white cat was very young and scared, so Bethany scooped her up and brought her home. She named her Little Havana.

Bethany felt Chloe had sent Little Havana to help heal her heart. What started as a powerful afterlife sign from Chloe ended in tragedy when Little Havana suddenly became very sick and died within a few days.

Bethany was crushed and did not understand why so many bad things kept happening.

Little Havana

First, losing Chloe and then Little Havana. That painful wound of grief had been reopened, and she felt even worse. Bethany needed answers, so she scheduled an appointment with me. She desperately needed to hear from Chloe.

As I opened the session, Chloe's energy came through with a wave of love. I felt every ounce of joy they had for each other.

"Chloe shows me a purple object and something else that sparkles and shines." I said, "I am not sure what it is, but it feels important. Do you know what this could be?"

There was only silence. I thought maybe our call had been disconnected when Bethany finally responded.

"I have two purple satin bags next to me with Chloe and Little Havana's ashes," Bethany said, "A Himalayan salt lamp and purple crystals are next to them."

"I can see it so clearly," I said, "Chloe shows me everything in detail."

I felt the energy surge as more messages came through.

"Chloe also shows me a green thing that is round like a spring," I continued, "Does this make sense?"

"Yes, I know what that is!" Bethany said. "Chloe's favorite toy is a little green spring. It is sitting right here too."

Bethany listened as Chloe described who she was with in the afterlife.

"I hear a name that starts with an L," I said, "Is there someone connected to you with an L name?"

Bethany had no idea who that could be but later learned from her mom about her Aunt Eloise, her grandmother's adopted sister, who passed away many years ago. Bethany told me later that this message shocked them because

Chloe sent information about a family member that Bethany did not know existed.

The following messages began to make more sense, which happens once I find the vibrational level I need to be on. It is a lot like tuning into a radio station. I sensed another human energy coming through with Chloe.

"Chloe is also with a grandfather figure," I said, "I see a farm in connection with your grandfather."

Bethany was suddenly very quiet. When she could finally speak, she confirmed that her departed grandfather lived on a farm. She found out later that Aunt Eloise was his sister-in-law.

"Chloe also says Ben is here and says to say *hi*," I said. "Who is Ben?"

Bethany was again speechless. Ben was her ex-father-in-law, who had also passed away.

There were a few other messages that we could not place, but that is normal and to be expected during a session. Usually, if something doesn't make sense, it is because of my error, such as not delivering the message correctly, or it may be an event in the future. In either case, there are always a few messages that we never figure out.

"Chloe also tells me she is with someone very special to you," I said, "She says this special someone needed to be loved for the last days of their life. Do you know who she is talking about?"

I had no idea at that time who that *special someone* was. I could feel the love and pure joy surrounding the message, so I knew it was a very important message.

Bethany suddenly burst into tears. She had always thought Chloe sent Little Havana to her but hearing it from me was the validation she desperately hoped for. Chloe knew Bethany would love and care for Little Havana during the last days of her life.

So much joy filled Bethany's heart. She knew that Chloe and Little Havana were together. Knowing they were not in pain but with loved ones in the afterlife was a relief. Chloe had one last message for Bethany.

"Chloe says she was ready to leave her body and is not upset about your decision to help her go," I said.

Bethany was overwhelmed with pure happiness when her session ended. She was finally able stop blaming herself. She thought she would never escape her dark place, but now her heart was open.

Whenever she starts to feel painful memories come back, she remembers Chloe's messages. She understands that every connection has purpose and meaning, no matter how brief.

With each passing day, Bethany is more grateful and appreciative than ever and lives with an open mind and heart thankful for the time she shared with her angels.

Chapter 54

Tyee

Tyee, also known as Ty, was a ten-year-old rat terrier and Italian greyhound mix with a short brown and white coat. Ellie felt a connection with Ty that was unlike any other dog.

He was a small, feisty dog with a big personality who never backed away from a challenge. Ty was fearless in his approach to life and always had a healthy appetite.

When he started losing interest in food and patches of fur came out, Ellie took him in for a check-up. She hoped it was just typical signs of aging. Further testing revealed Cushing's disease. Ellie had no idea how to manage this illness but was determined to keep Ty healthy.

Ellie researched everything she could find on the topic. She fed Ty special food and supplements and tried various alternative treatments; however, after several years and close monitoring, Ty's health declined.

Despite Ellie's efforts, it became clear that their time together was ending. Ellie and her husband, Jeremy, were devastated and, through their tears, made the impossible decision to say goodbye.

Ellie had never felt the grip of grief as deeply as she did after Ty took his last breath. She had devoted every waking moment to his care for the past fourteen years. The absence of Ty's presence was crushing.

He had been by her side through many milestones, including when she opened her specialty pet store, Lovable Pets, in Billings, Montana. Ty's role was Chief of Security, alerting when every customer walked in.

In the days following Ty's passing, Ellie was numb and unable to process the world around her. Everything seemed oddly out of sorts, and without Ty, the world seemed like a blank space. More than anything, she just wanted to know that Ty was okay and that he knew how much she loved and missed him.

Just two weeks after his transition, Ellie got an unexpected sign from Ty. She had just picked up his ashes and was emotionally drained. She wanted to clear her mind, so she went to the barn and saddled her horse, Melody. Ellie always felt a sense of comfort when she was with Melody, as if the horse had a magical grounding effect on her.

The corral was a welcome distraction, and Ellie noticed a hawk above her as they rode around it. It was a bit odd that the hawk did not seem to be concerned about their presence.

The hawk continued to circle her, and then it hovered so close she could see the eyes looking directly at her. It was a breathtaking moment; Ellie instantly connected to this bird.

She sensed Ty checking in on her and letting her know he was not the ashes she had just brought home. He was soaring like a hawk, flying effortlessly and free from his body. Ellie watched in amazement as the hawk eventually disappeared into the distance.

The whole experience made her feel lighter and brought a sense of peace to her broken heart. She wondered if Ty's spirit could have reached out to her.

After encountering the hawk, Ellie noticed birds around her more often than usual. Almost as if they were drawn to her. She also began to have vivid dreams about Ty that were so real, colorful, and unlike other dreams.

These experiences prompted her to search the internet for information about the afterlife of animals. Her search led her to order many books about the afterlife, including mine. When the books arrived, she devoured every word and was especially interested in the signs loved ones send from the afterlife.

Something clicked inside her when she finished reading my book. The stories resonated deeply and filled her with a sense of hope. She booked a session with me even though she was not entirely convinced that animal communication was real.

When I opened her session, Ty came through right away. His energy was light and perfectly balanced, and I could sense their strong connection.

"Ty tells me you are writing a book," I said. "He wants you to keep writing. He says it is important that your message goes out into the world. Do you understand this?"

Ellie was silent.

"I'm writing a book about him. Our story," Ellie said slowly.

As Ellie spoke, I saw Ty watching her write. It felt like he was guiding her hand. It was an incredible image of love.

"Ty is helping you write. He watches over you. He also wants to talk about sitting on a red deck," I said, "Do you know what he means?"

"I'm sitting outside right now on the deck," Ellie said, "It has a reddish-colored stain."

"Well, Ty is with you right now," I said as I saw his energy surround her like a hug. "He says your grandparents are here too, and I feel so much love around him."

Ellie was speechless. She loved her grandparents and was thrilled to know Ty was with them. There were many messages for Ellie's family that only they would know. Ty was determined to help Ellie through the pain.

What seemed impossible before was happening, and Ellie's world began to shift. For the first time since Ty's transition, Ellie felt a sense of joy in her heart. Each message that came through worked like magic and began to heal her broken heart.

This experience was the catalyst that prompted Ellie to embark on a spiritual journey that continues to this day. After our session, Ellie published her book, *Fly to Me; Extraordinary Lessons of Life and Death from a Little Dog.*

Writing their story was a pivotal part of Ellie's healing journey. The fact that Ty knew about it made it even more special. Their beautiful story captures their magical connection and Ty's ongoing presence in her life.

Ellie's life continues to transform. She opened a second location for her specialty pet store Lovable Pets, published her second book, *Laboratory Dogs Rescued: From Test Subjects to Beloved Companions,* and hosts a podcast, *Dog Research Exposed.*

Ellie continues to welcome rescued dogs into her home and has devoted her life to helping animals and being their voice.

That little dog gave Ellie the confidence to pursue her dreams and showed her how to live her life to the fullest and never back down from a challenge.

Ellie has found peace knowing her beloved Ty will always be right by her side as her trusted Chief of Security, announcing every customer that walks through the door.

Chapter 55

Argyle

When Danielle's West Highland terrier, Argyle, transitioned, she was inconsolable, so her friend Ellie from the previous chapter gave her a stack of books to help ease her pain.

She also sent her the recording from her session with Ty. Danielle was mesmerized by all the messages. Argyle was everything to her, and she desperately wanted to connect with him, so she promptly scheduled an appointment.

Before Danielle's appointment, I connected with Argyle to get to know him a little better and gain his trust.

I gazed at Argyle's photo and focused my energy. He had a short white coat, brown eyes, and his ears stood straight up. His head was slightly tilted as if he was listening to my words.

Suddenly, the image of a large glass of red wine appeared.

This is strange, I thought. *Why did he show me a glass of red wine?*

I asked Argyle to share more, but he was silent. It suddenly occurred to me that this may be something touchy such as an addiction or substance abuse. This happened in the past with other clients, which caused awkward tension.

Seeing a giant glass of red wine from a departed dog was unusual. I felt a sense of importance around the odd message, so I jotted it down in my notebook and hoped to get more information as the session progressed.

Danielle was excited and a bit nervous when she called for her appointment. She listened closely as I explained the process. Within moments, Argyle began sharing more details about himself. He was very chatty, so I tuned in to listen. Another unusual message came through.

"I normally don't hear things like this, but Argyle insists that I tell you he is very *competent*," I said. "Do you know what he means?"

Most dogs will share their favorite treats, toys, or memories. Argyle was making a bold statement about himself. He was *competent and proud of it.* Danielle immediately knew what he meant.

"Argyle was stubborn and wanted to do things his way," Danielle said, "If I was too overprotective, he would give me a look like, *Mom, I'm fine, let me run.* That sounds just like him."

"Okay," I said, "He is very proud of that. Now, Argyle says he is with a human male energy named *Robert.* He is holding Argyle," I said, "I see a pile of dogs around him, and he is so happy. Does this make sense?"

"Yes, it does," Danielle said, "Robert is my dad, and he just passed away. He loved dogs and had eleven of them at one time."

Hearing that her dad and Argyle were together brought Danielle great comfort, and I felt the energy shift.

"Argyle also shares the name *Mary* and a name that starts with the letter *A*," I said, "Do you know who he is referring to?"

"I do," Danielle said, "Mary is my mom, and Aaron is my brother. I also had my first dog, named Ami. It could be him too."

"It could be both your brother and Ami," I said, "Sometimes, one message includes more than one meaning. It is a way of saving energy. Kind of like a buy one, get one free type of thing."

It all seemed so unreal to Danielle. Argyle shared so many details about her life and her family. The grief she held so tightly in her heart started to be released.

Once again, Argyle showed me the glass of red wine, but I still didn't mention it. I could not get any more information from him, so I kept it to myself.

"Argyle talks about a white picket fence," I said, "Is this your home?"

"That was the last road trip we took together," Danielle said, "The campground had a white picket fence around it. We took our walks around the fence every day."

"He loved it there," I said, "He also tells me about a wrist or arm issue. Do you understand this?"

"That's my husband, Todd, who has tennis elbow," Danielle said, "He gets pretty painful."

Argyle continued to send messages, including a few that Danielle did not understand. Sometimes a client would contact me years later to tell me about a message that finally made sense. I told Danielle to file the information in her mind; hopefully, it would reveal itself someday.

As we were near the end of the session, Argyle showed me the giant glass of red wine again for the third time.

The animals often send the same message several times when it is important. This time I felt a sense of fame or celebrity around the message. It still didn't make any sense to me, but I have a rule I always follow during sessions. If I receive the same message three times, it must be important.

I finally relented and shared the odd message.

"Is there a reason Argyle would show me a large glass of red wine?" I asked. "He says he is a celebrity, and for some reason, he keeps showing me a huge glass of wine."

Danielle could not believe what she was hearing. After gathering her thoughts, she shared the significance of that message.

"On a recent road trip to the West Coast, we took Argyle to Dundee, Oregon, to visit the *Argyle Winery*," Danielle said, "The employees were thrilled by his name and treated him like royalty and dubbed him their mascot. We have photos in front of the *Argyle Winery* sign with Argyle surrounded by huge glasses of red wine! He loved every minute of the attention and celebrity status. I never posted the photos anywhere. Nobody knows about this except me and Todd."

Argyle knew. He was so proud of himself, and I was relieved that the odd message impacted Danielle so strongly.

Argyle's descriptive messages were the first step toward shifting Danielle's perspective from grief into healing. It was a slow but steady journey that started once she began to do the things she used to with Argyle.

Danielle consciously decided to stop the negative thoughts. Instead, she sent him love and talked to him daily. Danielle realized that Argyle never mentioned the discomfort and pain he struggled with for years.

When Argyle was about six years old, he started to act strangely. Danielle noticed that he would spin around as if something was attacking his hindquarters.

After numerous tests, it was confirmed that the cartilage of his rear knee had deteriorated. The strange behavior stemmed from Argyle's discomfort.

Danielle monitored him closely with medication and supplements; his well-being became her priority. Around the clock, she adjusted her daily life to ensure his comfort.

Despite his limitations, Argyle zoomed around like a young puppy wherever they went. He was happy and *competent,* determined to do things his way.

There was something about him that attracted the attention of strangers. He had charisma and charm that prompted people to stop and ask for his photo. Going for walks was always interesting as everyone wanted to meet Argyle. Of course, he loved the attention.

As the years passed, Argyle began to slow down. Danielle faced the grim reality of his mobility issues. She did everything she could to keep him comfortable. Soon after he turned fourteen, his liver began to fail, and he rapidly declined. Danielle held onto every moment they had.

Sadly within a short time his body could not take any more. Argyle transitioned peacefully at home, and Danielle's world came to a screeching halt.

Saying goodbye to Argyle felt like the destruction of her life. Danielle replayed everything in her mind. She agonized about her decisions, wondering if she could have done more.

She blamed herself for his sudden decline because she had just adjusted his medication. But the worst part was how guilty she felt for having to go to work and not being able to spend more time with him, especially during his final days.

Argyle did not talk about his death or anything negative about her decisions — only his strong personality and their happiest moments. Danielle was so relieved, and she could finally move forward, knowing those painful memories only belonged to her.

Motivated by that experience and wanting to know more about animal communication, Danielle became active in my practice group and learned to send and receive messages with Argyle.

That decision closed the gap in that massive hole in her heart. By following the simple steps of animal communication and actively tuning in, she started to receive messages from him.

She often feels his presence and dreams about him. They even developed a clever and musical way to communicate. Songs that hold powerful lyrics will play when she is driving.

The messages within the lyrics are often in sync with whatever is going on in her life. Each time, a wave of emotions confirms Argyle is near. Danielle can also smell his sweet fresh scent after his bath, and butterflies linger when they go camping.

She still misses him, but now instead of focusing on the negative, Danielle's thoughts hold only the deepest love.

She knows Argyle is alive and well in spirit, and their bonds of love are so strong they will always be connected.

Chapter 56

Chloe and Baby Jojo

Chloe

Karen felt a part of her died when she had to say goodbye to her beloved cats, Chloe and Baby Jojo.

They transitioned within a short time of each other, and this was the worst loss she had ever endured. In her mind, nothing was going to bring her peace.

Little did she know her angel cats were hard at work guiding her to someone who could help her find her smile again.

Chloe was a sixteen-year-old white cat with long fur and green eyes. She was diagnosed with an aggressive form of cancer, and Karen and her husband, Mark, did their best to support her during grueling rounds of chemotherapy.

Within a few months, Chloe's condition worsened, and they made that impossible decision to say goodbye. They had recently lost their other cats, Gossamer and Panache, and their hearts were again torn apart.

Their last remaining cat, Baby Jojo, had been healthy his entire life. He had short white fur and blue eyes and loved to be carried like a baby. Without warning, Baby Jojo collapsed and had to be rushed to the emergency clinic.

He spent the next few days in the clinic in critical condition. As the days passed, Baby Jojo's condition declined.

Despite their efforts, he passed away at sixteen from complications stemming from pancreatitis.

Struggling with the pain of two losses, Karen could barely function. The days ran together, feeling empty and meaningless.

She attended group therapy and was introduced to an animal communicator at one of their meetings. Her session made her feel worse because it was generic and could have been applied to anyone.

Nothing seemed to help, so Karen searched for animal communicators who were also evidential mediums and found my website.

An evidential medium specializes in delivering specific and factual information during a session. Karen read the testimonials, and something inside clicked. She hoped she would finally get the detailed messages confirming that her beloved cats were alive and well in the afterlife.

As she scheduled the session online, Karen thought only a miracle could stop the pain, but she was willing to try again.

With much anticipation, her appointment finally arrived. The miracle Karen was hoping for was delivered in the very first message.

I opened the session with Baby Jojo and focused on his energy. I only had his name and photograph. Baby Jojo came through loud and clear. I immediately sensed his excitement and was overwhelmed by a wave of loving energy.

"Baby Jojo's energy is coming through quickly," I said, "He is very excited about his *ears*. He is jumping up and down and pointing to his ears. I have never had a cat show this much excitement about its ears. Is there a reason he would be so happy about them?"

Karen was shocked. She gathered her thoughts and explained how important that message was.

"Baby Jojo was born deaf," Karen said, "That's why he is so excited about his ears. He was deaf but now he can hear!"

She knew from her research that any illnesses or medical issues disappear when animals transition from their body. Baby Jojo was whole again. That was the most powerful message and extraordinary validation that he was alive and well in the afterlife.

From that moment, Karen's grief started to lift. Even though I am conducting the session, I feel the release of pain too.

There was a whirlwind of detailed messages that continued to come through from Baby Jojo that provided many validations.

I closed the session, returned his energy, and invited Chloe to come forward. Once again, the messages came through with abundant love and evidential messages.

"I am not sure who this goes to," I said, "But Chloe tells me that someone very close to you has tragic mobility issues."

I heard a gasp over the phone and then total silence.

"My mom," Karen said, "We are very close. She suffers from a debilitating disease centered around balance, causing her to fall and have ongoing mobility issues."

Chloe shared many more messages that day that were profoundly healing. When the grief lifts, the messages flow more freely.

I could feel how much lighter my office felt. To be a part of Karen's transformation is a powerful force. There is truly nothing that compares to this experience.

It has been many years since Karen and I had a session together, but the messages remain as clear as the day I delivered them. She is a different person because of her experience.

Before her session, Karen struggled daily with grief and had lost all hope. The pain had taken over her life.

Her cats guided her on this path of discovery and led her to my website. Our departed loved ones know who can help us in times of turmoil. They silently witness our lives and gently nudge us along the way.

Even though her losses never leave her, Karen is confident that she will someday be reunited with her beloved cats again.

Her heart has a new sense of calmness, a reason to wake up every morning. While she misses their physical presence, she knows her beloved cats are all right by her side.

Chapter 57

Maya

Kenya had never thought about the afterlife or animal communication, but she had to find some way to work through her grief. She wanted to know that death had not ended her lifelong connection to her sixteen-year-old white Maltese, Maya.

Kenya researched pet loss online and found a social media group where someone mentioned my book. Fascinated,

Kenya devoured the chapters and was especially drawn to read about the signs pets send from the afterlife.

She had not received any signs from Maya but was intrigued by the possibility and made a mental note of what to watch for.

Shortly after Kenya read the chapter about afterlife signs, she was driving to see a client when she noticed the car in front of her had a personalized license plate. As she approached the car, she could not believe her eyes.

The four letters, M A Y A, came clearly into focus. Kenya was thrilled and immediately thanked Maya for sending that sign.

The chances of that name being right in front of her were staggering.

There would be more signs to follow.

One day, she saw movement out of the corner of her eye and saw Maya's tail going toward the doggy bed. It was a partial apparition and had all the distinctive characteristics of her tail.

The size, shape, and color were precisely like Maya's tail. Kenya checked the area, but there was no one there.

Another time Maya made her presence known was when Kenya's sister visited. Kenya felt something brush past her ankle as she opened the front door. Kenya looked down, but no one was there.

Her sister asked what she was looking at, and she said, "Maya is here. I just felt her!"

It was shortly after these incidences that Kenya booked an appointment with me.

Kenya called in on the recorded line with anticipated excitement. With only Maya's photo and her basic information, I opened the session with a powerful mantra and blessing.

Maya's energy came through so quickly.

"I see Maya with several other little dogs," I said, "She is smiling and so sweet. Maya is very excited to be here and loves you so much."

"Yes," Kenya said, "I have several little dogs that have passed away, so it makes sense they are all together."

"I also see a gray car. Maya is sitting in the front passenger seat with two other little dogs," I said, "I'm not sure why the car is significant. Does this make sense to you?"

There was total silence.

Kenya gained her composure and said, "I can't believe this. I am in my gray car right now. I wanted to go somewhere for my session where it would be quiet and peaceful, so I drove my car to the park. I lost two of my other dogs, Julie, and Little Daisy. They were both rescues that I got when they were older. They would all be together again now. They are here with me now?"

"Yes, they are beside you in the passenger seat," I said. "I see all three of them."

Kenya listened in awe as I described the dogs.

"Maya also tells me you have another Maltese that resembles her. Is that correct?" I asked.

"Yes! I have another Maltese. She was my first dog as an adult," Kenya said.

The following message was a bit odd.

"Maya keeps talking about turtles," I said, "She is not telling me anything about them. Do you understand this?"

Kenya thought about that message, but the only thing that came to her was that one of her clients had several turtles.

Kenya did not understand that message or why Maya would mention the turtles in her care but promised to let me know if it made sense later.

I delivered many other loving messages from Maya and gently closed the session.

A few days later, Kenya was in her home office, and her husband, Alfredo, came in and looked around the room.

"Where are the turtles I gave you?" Alfredo asked.

Kenya stopped what she was doing and stared at him in shock.

Alfredo always brought Kenya little gifts from the airport when he traveled. After Maya's passing, he gave her three little decorative turtles.

She displayed them on a shelf in her office. She had recently moved things around, and the turtles were in another location.

That was it!

The turtle message!

Maya had to be with her to know she had just moved them. Kenya's heart overflowed with joy.

After her session, Kenya finally worked through the grief and released the guilt that held her hostage for so long.

It was a long and painful journey, but this experience with Maya opened many new doors for her. She knows that when she is quiet and meditates, she can ask for signs from her departed pets.

Now, Kenya lives her life in the present moment. The strong bonds she and Maya shared guided her to seek answers to her questions and be open to manifesting what she wants.

Maya will always be with her, watching over her.

Kenya asked the Universe for happiness, and the Universe delivered.

Chapter 58

Lahli

Lahli was a Siamese cat with a short cream-colored coat, a black mask, and blue eyes. She was very dignified and became the supreme ruler of Judy's home. Only the sound of the ironing board unfolding would send her scrambling into a panic.

Judy saw her photo on a flier at her veterinarian's office as a two-year-old cat needing a home. She immediately sensed they were meant to be together. Her bright blue eyes cast a much older and wiser soul than her young age reflected.

Their bond grew so strong that it was as if they had known each other in past lifetimes. Later during one of our many sessions together, Lahli shared many of those experiences with me. They had quite a history together.

When Judy discovered Lahli had cancer, she scheduled a session with me to check on her level of comfort.

I connected with Lahli and immediately sensed her energy was dwindling. Like turning the flame down on the stove, her inner light was dim compared to previous sessions.

Lahli was very clear that she was ready to leave her body. She was so calm about her upcoming transition and at peace with her beautiful life. Judy was overcome with sadness but relieved to know how Lahli felt.

Judy arranged to say goodbye at home, creating a quiet and calm space for Lahli. She had been such a joy for seventeen years that she deserved dignity and peace. Judy arranged powerful spiritual artifacts and holy water around her. She held her gently and softly chanted sacred mantras as Lahli took her last breath.

The next few weeks blurred together, and the tears never stopped. Lahli was not just a pet but a magical, mystical, old soul. Judy felt a part of her soul left with Lahli, and only sorrow remained.

Judy was desperate to connect with Lahli, so she scheduled an afterlife session. Before Judy called for her appointment, I opened a space for Lahli to join me. I was taken aback by how velvety smooth Lahli's energy came through.

She glowed and smiled with her eyes and stood about six feet tall. As Judy's call came in, I watched in awe as Lahli's energy excitedly zipped around the room.

"I'm so excited to hear from Lahli," Judy said, "Please ask her if she intends to come back and if she will be a dog or a cat."

Lahli was quick to respond.

"Lahli said she *will always be a cat*," I said, "She is very clear about that but offers no other details about reincarnation."

I sharpened my focus as another message came through.

"Lahli tells me she is a guide in the afterlife," I said.

"Oh, for pets?" Judy asked.

"Not only for you but for other humans and animals," I said.

"I believe that. She is so wise," Judy said. She had always sensed that Lahli was her primary spirit guide.

"Can she tell you anything about dancing?" Judy asked.

"Lahli says if you can call *that* dancing," I said, "She thinks that is funny."

Lahli's response made us both laugh out loud.

Judy shared a story about how Lahli refused to be held, and the only time she would allow it was when they danced together in her apartment.

Judy would play the song, *Soothe Me, Baby*, by Rod Stewart, and she would pick Lahli up and dance around dipping her as if they were dance partners. I could see them dancing as Judy spoke.

"Lahli wants me to talk about the noodles," I said. "Do you understand this?" I was not sure about that message but had come to trust Lahli's accuracy.

"She loved noodles!" Judy said excitedly. "I just had ramen noodles last night, which was her favorite. For some reason, she loved to eat those noodles."

Judy was ecstatic. No one knew about Lahli's passion for ramen noodles.

"Now, this next message is strange," I said, "Lahli wants me to talk about a gerbil or a rat in a box. I see a name that starts with a J, but it's not you, Judy. Do you know anyone with a J name and a pet rat or gerbil?"

We both chuckled at the odd question, and nothing came to Judy's mind. I turned my focus back to Lahli.

"She shows me an Ireland connection. Do you have any ties to Ireland?" I asked.

"No," Judy said, "But I'll think about that and let you know."

"Okay, please do," I said.

Suddenly, I felt another presence. A human male spirit stepped forward and told me his name starts with P, as in Paul. I felt this man was concerned for someone's health and wanted to share this urgent message.

"He says, *don't do as I did, do as I say, don't smoke.* Then he points to his throat," I said. "Do you know who this is or what this means?"

Judy had no clue what it meant but promised to get back to me if she figured it out.

Hearing Lahli's messages was just what she needed. Judy laughed for the first time since Lahli passed, and it felt so good.

After that session, Judy thought about the Ireland connection. She had a friend who was Irish. Perhaps that man was connected to her, so she called *Shannon O'Reilly* and asked her if she understood the messages.

When she heard Shannon's response, Judy was speechless.

Shannon's Uncle Paul died of lung cancer. He was a heavy smoker. Shannon's daughter was just diagnosed with stage four lung cancer.

The message, *don't do as I did, do as I say, don't smoke,* hit the mark for Shannon's family.

That mystery was solved, but we still didn't know the message about the rat or gerbil.

A few weeks later, Judy emailed with exciting news. Her friend, *Joyce,* was the only one she could think of with a name that started with a J. Judy contacted her and asked if she had a pet gerbil or rat.

Her response was right on target.

"Well, yes, that must be my daughter Samantha's rat," Joyce said. "She found a box in the dumpster and heard something inside. She opened the box and found a rat. It was still alive, and we think it was intended to be food for a snake. She kept the rat as a pet and still has it."

This was absolutely amazing. It took Judy a few weeks of research to determine what those messages meant.

It was incredible that Lahli sent information Judy knew nothing about. Those messages were truly remarkable.

It has been over ten years since Lahli transitioned, and Judy misses her daily companionship. Judy often senses Lahli's presence near her, primarily when she conducts healing sessions, so she remains open to learning all she can from her.

Lahli has taught Judy so much about life and how animals see things differently than we do. Animals approach the end of life with acceptance and peace.

Experiencing such profound grief was so hard, but it allowed Judy to understand how much Lahli meant to her.

She knows they will always be connected, just as they were in their many past lives.

Until then, Judy trusts that Lahli is leading her spirit team and watching over her as her guardian angel.

Chapter 59

Cassie

Cassie was Carolyn's fourteen-year-old collie and German shepherd mix. She had medium-length black wavy fur with brown on her legs, under her neck, and two perfect brown eyebrows.

She was the center of Carolyn's life and her constant companion. As the years passed, Cassie began to show signs of aging. Her legs were getting weaker, causing her to slip on the floors, so Carolyn put rugs all over the house so Cassie would not fall.

Cassie's health continued to decline, and soon she had trouble swallowing and could not keep her food down. The tests revealed a mass in her throat, and the prognosis was not good. Carolyn was devastated and overwhelmed by the thought of losing her. She did her best to care for Cassie and keep her comfortable.

Then one day, Carolyn looked into Cassie's eyes and knew it was time. She had promised Cassie, she would not keep her here too long. But that did not make it any easier.

It was inconceivable that she had to make such a horrible decision. It did not feel right even though it was the best thing for Cassie. Carolyn and her boyfriend, Al, surrounded Cassie with love and said goodbye.

Every day the grief and sorrow increased. From numbness to sharp pain, it all seemed surreal. She could not believe that Cassie was gone.

One day, Carolyn went outside on the deck to clear her mind. She noticed something on the chair.

In the middle of the cushion, perfectly placed, was a beautiful white feather. In awe, Carolyn picked up the feather and wondered if Cassie had sent it to her. The grief welled up instantly. Carolyn was soon lost in tears and memories.

A few days later, Carolyn visited her mom and told her about the feather she found on the deck chair. Her mom gave her a book about the afterlife, hoping it would ease her pain.

Carolyn was enthralled and wanted to learn more. She had never thought about an afterlife for pets before but always believed in angels.

An online search led her to my books which she quickly ordered. Fascinated by the stories, she booked an afterlife session with me.

As I waited for Carolyn's call, I created a space for Cassie's energy to come through. It is like opening a virtual doorway in space and time.

I felt a surge of positive energy, and Cassie appeared before me. Sometimes I see the animal's face or eyes, and other times I see its entire body. I never know what to expect.

Cassie looked gorgeous. She was smiling and shimmering with light. She bounced around joyfully and wanted to play with me. She had a ball in her mouth, which she kept bringing to me, but she would not let it go.

I played a game of keep away with Cassie until Carolyn's call came through.

"This is so cute. Cassie is playing keep away with me," I said, "She brings the ball to me with a big smile, but she won't give it to me. She also shows me how she runs by the water. Does this make sense?"

"That's her!" Carolyn said, "We live by the beach and walk by the water all the time. She always had her ball in her mouth and would never drop it."

"There is so much joy around her," I said, "She shows me how well you cared for her. She had the best of everything."

"Cassie was always so happy. When we built our home, we considered Cassie's needs in the floor plan," Carolyn said. "We made it easy for her to access the yard as she aged."

Suddenly, I could see the world through Cassie's eyes. I saw flashes of her life and every room in the house. I described each in detail as if I were floating above them.

"Cassie shows me a loft. I see her looking down through the railing," I said, "There is a fireplace in the living room below."

"Yes!" Carolyn said, "We have a landing upstairs that overlooks the living room. She loved to sleep there."

"Cassie wants me to talk about her fur. Something special about it," I said. "I am not sure what that means, but it is very important."

"After she died, my vet snipped a swatch of her fur. I have it as a keepsake." Carolyn said. "I hold onto it when I'm missing her."

"She knows you do that. She also wants me to talk about her paw," I said. "Is there anything that comes to mind? I don't know if it is a health issue or something else."

"After Cassie died, I got a tattoo of her name and paw prints on my wrist," Carolyn said. "That's amazing she can see it."

When Carolyn realized Cassie knew about the tattoo, everything fell into sync. It amazed me how Cassie knew exactly what Carolyn needed to hear. The power of love began to fill the void in Carolyn's heart. I finished the session with more messages then gently sent Cassie's energy back.

I felt the grief melt away as Cassie shared those life-changing messages. That session opened a spiritual door and more signs from Cassie continued to appear as if by magic.

Carolyn found five feathers that have no logical explanation. She does not have pet birds or feather pillows. One time she opened her car door, and there was a feather right where she would step. Another time, she was home, and a feather slowly drifted down in front of her face from the ceiling.

For Carolyn, it is genuinely heartwarming and surprising at the same time. She is grateful for every sign and thanks Cassie for sending them.

After her session, Carolyn opened her heart again to love again. She was thrilled when her new dogs displayed Cassie's personality and unique behavior.

Carolyn's experience made her a better mom with her new dogs and helped her develop a closer bond with them. A new sense of peace fills the void where once there was only pain knowing her angel, Cassie, would always be right by her side.

Chapter 60

Butterscotch and Cowboy

Cindee and Bob scheduled a session with me for their beloved cat, Butterscotch, who recently transitioned from age-related kidney disease. Butterscotch was one of two kittens dumped on a family member's property when they were just ten weeks old. Butterscotch and his littermate, Bobaloo, were tabbies with long orange and white striped fur, often called ginger tabbies.

Cindee felt Butterscotch's presence around her numerous times. She was thinking about him one day and glanced out the window. A cloud formed in the shape of Butterscotch lying down with his beautiful fur cascading down around his neck.

Another time, her husband, Bob, ended a call, and Butterscotch's photo randomly popped up.

Cindee also felt his presence when her water bottle was tipped over for no apparent reason.

They often felt a cat lying between them at night when no cat was there. Obviously, Butterscotch wanted his mom and dad to know he was with them.

Cindee called for her appointment, and I opened the session with Butterscotch. His energy came through quickly, and he was so polite and gentlemanly.

I gazed into his gorgeous yellow eyes and told him how handsome he was. He showed me luxurious lion's fur and began sending numerous messages.

"Butterscotch says he has luxurious *lion's fur*," I said, "I told him how handsome he was, and he sent me an image of a lion."

"I called him my lion king," Cindee said, "No one knows that except me and Bob!"

"He loves that name," I said, "I can feel the love when you say it."

The waves of energy during a session are so powerful. Unless you experience it for yourself, it is difficult to explain the intensity. It is like getting goosebumps on top of goosebumps. Like goosebumps on steroids.

"Butterscotch shows me a pineapple," I said, "Do you know what this is about?"

"Pineapple?" Cindee said, "I know exactly what that is. I just bought a pineapple slicer. It was just delivered and is on the counter right now. I don't know why I ordered it. I like pineapple, but I hardly ever buy it. One of those impulsive online purchases I made."

"Oh, that is too funny!" I said, "He must have seen you order it. He brings a human spirit into the session. It is a female with a name that starts with the letter *J or G*. Do you know who this may be?

"Yes!" Cindee said, "That's my Aunt Jean!"

"Wait, there is another person here," I said, "Another female with Butterscotch. Her name starts with an *M.*"

"That's my great Aunt, Mae-Mi," Cindee said, "My Aunt Jean's aunt. She told me about her, but I never knew her."

Knowing Butterscotch was with her loved ones gave Cindee peace of mind, and the pain from her loss started to lift. I finished the session and sent everyone's energy back.

There was a sense of peace when Cindee hung up the phone.

I will never get tired of feeling that.

Cowboy

A few days after their twelve-year-old tri-colored Bernese mountain dog mix named Cowboy transitioned, Cindee got up early one morning and felt something soft under her foot.

She glanced down and saw a wide green cloth ribbon cascading down from the top of a six-foot-tall cabinet in the bedroom.

The ribbon was wrapped around the storage box it was in and draped across the cabinet to the floor. It looked as if someone had perfectly arranged it.

Cindee stared in disbelief at the ribbon, trying to make sense of it. Neither she nor Bob had moved any items on that cabinet.

It would have been impossible for anyone to get that spool of ribbon out of the box and arrange it without them noticing it.

This ribbon was Cindee's favorite, and she instantly knew it was a sign from Cowboy.

It would be just like him to move something she loved to let them know he was still there.

That sign from Cowboy was a welcome relief and helped ease their pain, as his transition was an unexpected shock. They had found him unconscious in their home and rushed him to the nearest emergency clinic.

Sadly, Cowboy was gone by the time they arrived. Bob and Cindee were overcome with sadness at the loss of their gentle boy. Cindee felt she should have known something was wrong and was wrought with guilt.

Cowboy's timely sign from the afterlife was exactly what Cindee needed. Unexplained events continued to occur around the house. One night before bed, Bob glanced at his calculator and saw two characters on the screen. The letters *H I.*

When the lights dim by themselves or missing objects suddenly appear, their hearts fill with joy. They know it is another sign that their beloved companions are still with them.

Chapter 61

Rocco

Several months after Russell's miniature schnauzer, Rocco, transitioned, his mom, Gena, gifted him an afterlife session with me. Gena was a client of mine and knew a message from Rocco would help her son heal.

Russell and his husband, Sam, fell in love with Rocco when he was just eight weeks old. They searched for the perfect puppy, and to their delight, an eight-week-old miniature schnauzer found them.

There was a litter with ten miniature schnauzers, but only one stole their heart. The little salt and pepper-colored puppy jumped into their arms and crawled all over them, so the choice was obvious. They named him Rocco, and he would become the greatest joy in their life.

They went everywhere together, and one of Rocco's favorite things was to roll in the rosemary bushes when they went for a walk. Rocco was happy, loving, loyal, and always snuggled beside Russell when he slept.

When Rocco was about twelve, Russell took him in for a follow-up appointment after finding some fatty tumors on his lower back. The doctor also recommended an ultrasound. Russell left Rocco at the clinic and went home to wait for an update.

The call from the doctor came as a shock and turned into Russell's worst nightmare.

The results confirmed Rocco had a cancerous liver. The cancer was so advanced the prognosis was bleak. Other than normal aging, they had no indications of any underlying health issues.

What was meant to be a routine check-up turned into Rocco's last moments on Earth. They had no option but to let him go while he was under sedation. Russell and Sam never got to say goodbye to their sweet boy.

The aftermath of losing Rocco was utter devastation. Russell withdrew from family and friends. He missed several months of work and slipped into a dark place of pain.

Russell silently wished he would die to be with Rocco. He lost something so precious nothing mattered to him anymore.

When Russell's appointment with me arrived, he did not believe anything would ease his pain, but he was willing to try. He believed in animal communication, so this was his chance to tell Rocco how much he loved and missed him.

When I opened the session with Rocco, I felt a surge of loving energy. Like a wave of joy, gratitude, and pure happiness all rolled into one.

I shared those emotions with Russell trying to find the right words to describe how much love I felt. Rocco began to send a series of words and images.

"The first thing Rocco shows me is the shower," I said, "He says there is something significant about being in the shower. Do you understand this?"

"Yes, I do!" Russell said, "The first time Rocco barked was when I was in the shower. A big bark came out of his tiny body. That was a big moment for us that we talked about all the time. We will never forget it."

Animals love to share special moments like this. It is always such a blessing that they highlight their life's most positive and funny moments. Rarely do they mention anything sad.

"Now, this is a bit odd," I said, "Rocco wants to talk about something he says is *jammy, like grapes.* That is an unusual word. Do you have any idea what *jammy* means?"

Russell thought for a moment.

"I know what that is," Russell said, "Rocco loved wine. He would sit beside me while I was drinking wine and stare at the glass. He loved it, and I always let him lick the glass when I was done."

"Well, no wonder I had no idea what he meant," I said, "I asked him several times, but all I heard was *say jammy*. How cute is that?"

If animals don't know the word for something, they either make up a word or flash an image of the object. Rocco came up with the word *jammy* to describe wine.

"He keeps telling me about something with an herbal scent," I said, "What would this be?"

"Rosemary!" Russell said, "He loved to roll in the rosemary bush on our walks and smelled like it all day. That is his signature scent."

In just two messages, the energy shifted, and I could feel the heaviness lifting from Russell. Many more messages came through, some with a few laughs and some with a few tears. It was a beautiful reunion and the energy felt so balanced.

"The last thing Rocco is telling me is there is something different about your eyes," I said, "Have your eyes changed? Do you understand this?"

I heard Russell gasp on the phone.

"My glasses!" he said excitedly, "I wear glasses now. When Rocco was alive, I wore contacts. He has never seen me in glasses. He's here. Rocco is really here!"

What may be a seemingly insignificant reference to eyes or wine is the exact message Russell needed to hear. The grief lifted as soon as he realized Rocco was still with him. It was amazing to witness, and I am always honored to be a part of this process.

Russell talks to Rocco daily, and in doing so, he has activated his natural abilities for animal communication. With his new perspective about the afterlife, Russell set his goal to become a professional animal communicator so he can deliver healing messages to other distraught pet parents too.

Chapter 62

Riley

Riley was a tri-colored Australian shepherd. Her face had a black mask, white muzzle, brown eyebrows, and cheeks. She was usually a happy, easy-going girl, but at twelve, she had not been herself, so Liza took her to the vet for a check-up.

When an ultrasound found a tumor on her spleen, Liza and her boyfriend, Leland, faced the grim reality that their time with their sweet girl was quickly coming to an end.

Liza had never had to decide on euthanasia, and it felt horribly wrong. The doctor informed them it was the only option. Riley would not make it through the night. They tearfully held her close as Riley took her last breath.

Liza and Leland barely made it home from the vet's office. They were so overcome with emotion. Distraught and deeply grieving, neither could function, and they stayed home and cried for days.

It was so different than losing a human loved one. Riley was a part of every aspect of their life. She was the first face they saw in the morning and the last at night. Now, she was gone, and everything felt so empty.

Liza's boss showed little compassion when she returned to work.

"Are you okay?" her boss asked.

Liza burst into tears.

"Wow," her boss said, "You're not okay. It's been three days. Why are you crying?"

This is so common and unfortunate. Losing a beloved companion is often downplayed, and many do not understand the depth of the pain. Heartless employers need to realize the incapacitating grief that follows the loss of a beloved companion can be even deeper than a human loss. No one has the right to measure pain.

Liza and Leland struggled with their loss and watched helplessly while their other dog, Cooper, relentlessly searched for Riley throughout the house.

With the holidays coming up, Liza felt detached from the customary celebrations. She had no desire to decorate, or wrap presents and felt like a piece of her heart was torn out.

All their despair was about to change.

Thankfully, Liza's family was very supportive and understood the pain they felt. Liza's sister, Tara, gave her an afterlife session with me as a gift. Liza was thrilled and anxiously awaited her upcoming appointment.

As I opened the session, I immediately sensed Riley's energy swirling in excitement.

The very first message from Riley came through.

"Riley says she was in the store with you when you were looking at the turtles," I said, "Does that make any sense to you?"

At first, Liza thought, *turtles? I don't have any turtles.* But then it hit her.

"Oh, my gosh," Liza said, "I know what that is. I was at the drugstore with Leland, browsing the candy aisle as he waited for a prescription. There was a display with boxes of chocolate candies called *Turtles.* I had never seen them before, but I love candy, so I bought a box."

No one knew she bought a box of turtle candies. Liza was even more amazed that Riley was with her as she browsed the aisles. She was not thinking about Riley in that drugstore, so it was interesting that Riley was still with her.

I sharpened my focus as more messages came through.

"Riley is with a dog whose name starts with an *S*, like Sam, and another dog with an L name, like Larry," I said. "Do you know who they are?"

"Yes!" Liza said, "That's my dog Sam and my sister's dog, Louie! They are all together! Oh my gosh!"

It is fun to know who our companions are with in the afterlife. Sometimes it is another animal, and other times it can be a human. In this case, it was clear they were all having fun because everyone was smiling.

"Riley shows me a bowl of bones," I said. "Do you understand this?"

"I do!" Liza said, "Riley's food bowl was white with little black bones decorated around it."

Riley continued to share images of their favorite places at the beach and the mountains. Liza's pain was replaced with joy and pure happiness.

The energy had shifted, and the grief began to lift like magic.

Riley shared more messages, and I gently closed the session.

Liza has continued to receive signs from all her beloved dogs. When she lost her black border collie, Henry, she felt peace knowing Riley and the others would be there to greet him.

Liza will often see the numbers 205 and 502.

Henry was born on February 5th, and Riley on May 2nd.

Liza will ask for a sign when she is driving, and within a short time she will see a license plate or address with those numbers.

There is no cure for grief. But a message from the afterlife sure helps to ease the pain. Liza finally released all the negative emotions that weighed so heavily upon her and welcomed joy back into her heart. Liza and Leland made a conscious decision to celebrate every day with gratitude and joy knowing Riley and all their companions were still connected and part of their life.

Chapter 63

Sammy

Sammy was an eight-week-old Yorkshire terrier and poodle mix who fit into the palm of Missy's hand. He had wavy black fur with one white spot over his heart.

Sammy was the perfect playmate for Emma, his sibling from another litter. Emma was a bit smaller with solid black fur. The two pups bonded instantly as if they knew they were related.

Sammy and Emma were inseparable and had to be near each other constantly. They were never left alone because Missy took the dogs to her mom's house whenever she had errands. Her mom lived two houses away, and the pups loved visiting their grandma.

Sammy had been healthy throughout his adult life, with one exception. He had bladder stones which were removed a few years earlier. Missy didn't think much about it then, but after a trip to the beach when he was about twelve, she knew something was wrong when Sammy would not eat.

When the doctor told her his kidney values were high, Missy was shocked. He had not known any symptoms to that point.

They began treatments and flushed his kidneys daily at the clinic. Missy and her husband, David, settled into a routine of daily trips to the clinic.

David was close to Sammy, and despite the ongoing care, they both noticed Sammy was still not himself. Sammy's kidney enzymes were even higher at the two-week check-up. This was not the news they wanted to hear. Sammy was declining rapidly.

With the impossible decision to say goodbye looming over them, David, Missy, and their daughter Hannah gathered around him. Hannah whispered gently to him as she always did. Sammy took his last breath and peacefully left his body.

There was so much guilt around the decision to end his life. It was the only option, but it still felt wrong. The depth of pain was overwhelming for Missy and David. There were days when all they could do was cry.

Instead of holding back the pain, they decided to release it. One day they were furniture shopping, and they both got emotional thinking about Sammy. With strangers watching, David and Missy broke down in sobs.

They embraced their grief which helped ease their pain.

Missy had always believed in the afterlife and excitedly booked a session with me.

When I prepare for a session, I am aware of subtle changes around me. Animal energy feels different than human energy, and I sensed a human spirit waiting with Sammy.

I opened the session with Sammy and sensed his deep love for his family.

"Sammy wants me to acknowledge a military-type person," I said, "There is a military uniform, but I also see a badge for law enforcement, so I am not quite sure which it was. Are you familiar with anyone like this?"

"That's my husband," Missy said, "He and Sammy were close. He was in the air force and worked in law enforcement."

"Sammy says he is being spoiled rotten by another male energy named Gabriel," I said, "This man is laughing and smiling and kissing Sammy all over his face. Do you know who this is?"

"Yes, I do!" Liza said, "That's my friend, Gabriel. He loved Sammy and sadly died in a car accident when Sammy was about two years old.

"He is catching up on lost time now with Sammy now," I said, "They are both smiling and having fun."

The messages continued to come through.

"Sammy wants me to talk about Hannah," I said, "He says she is his angel. He loved it when Hannah held him and whispered to him. It made him feel so loved. Do you know who this is?"

"Yes!" Missy said with excitement, "Hannah is my daughter. She loved Sammy and always held and whispered to him like that."

"Now, Sammy says to talk about someone in a wheelchair," I said, "The message he has for them is, *I love you, and I am always with you.*"

"Yes, that's my mom," Missy said, "She lives two houses away, and he spent a lot of time with her. She has a wheelchair, but she hasn't used it."

"He sure loves his grandma," I said, "He keeps repeating the message, so it must be important."

Less than two weeks after this message was delivered, Missy's mom, who was eighty-six, fell and broke her leg. She had to have surgery, spent the next six months in bed, and needed a wheelchair for rehabilitation.

She would never walk again.

Somehow Sammy foretold the future.

"Okay, now he says *green beans,*" I said, "He is making a disgusting face but thinks it is funny all at the same time. Does that make sense?"

Missy explained how Sammy's sister, Emma had diabetes, so she had to switch from the turkey bacon snacks to a healthier option.

So instead of changing Emma's snacks, she gave all the dogs green beans.

Sammy ate them initially but spat them onto the floor afterward.

This was surprising because Sammy loved everything except green beans.

There were many more messages from Sammy, such as the candle Missy lit for him, a recent shopping trip to choose new flooring, a vivid dream about him, and jewelry she had made in his image. But the last message was beyond what Missy could have imagined.

"Sammy keeps saying the words *baby boy, baby boy*," I said, "Is this a name you called him? I'm not sure what this is."

"No," Missy said, "I didn't call him that. I'm not sure either, but I'll think about it."

Ten months later, Missy's daughter, Hannah, gave birth to a baby boy.

Sammy's messages were pivotal in lifting the grief which loomed over Missy and David. He made sure everyone he cared about knew they were loved. Knowing he was alive and well in spirit was a soothing relief.

They know Sammy is happy and always near; one day, they will see him again.

Just leave the green beans behind.

Chapter 64

Doc

Deidra dropped Doc off at the training facility when an unsettling sense of dread washed over her. She tried to convince herself everything would be okay, and Doc would be home in a few weeks. Dedria had no idea she would never see him alive again.

He'll be fine, she said to herself. *Nothing terrible will happen.*

Doc Holliday was a two-year-old silver Labrador retriever who weighed about one hundred pounds.

Silver Labradors are less common than other retrievers and have coats with a pale silvery gray hue. Doc was healthy, athletic, and full of energy.

The plan was to let Doc settle in for the night and begin training the following day.

A frantic call from the trainer came through early in the morning.

"I don't know how to tell you this," he said, "Doc is dead. I went to his kennel to work with him this morning, and he was dead. I am so sorry."

The trainer's voice trailed off as Dedria's world turned upside down.

They had no idea what happened. Doc was in his kennel alone, and there were no signs of any injuries. Those feelings of dread Dedria had now made sense.

She immediately blamed herself for his death, as she was the one who dropped him off at the training facility. Doc might still be alive if she had just listened to her instincts.

Consumed by her tragic loss, Dedria searched online for answers to help her through the numbing pain. She ordered several books, including mine, and devoured every word. She read the chapters about afterlife signs, and something clicked in her mind.

Shortly after Doc died, multiple butterflies fluttered around her. One of them followed her around the yard just like Doc used to do.

Another time, a butterfly landed on her hand and rode with her on her all-terrain vehicle. These random and unexplainable encounters spurred Dedria to book an afterlife session with me.

As I opened the session, I felt Doc's powerful energy come through like a freight train.

"Doc tells me your loved ones greeted him in the afterlife. He talks about the spirit energy of a grandmother with a name that starts with an M A, like Maggie," I said. "Do you have a grandmother with a name like that?"

"Yes, I do! Both of my grandmothers have MA names. One is Mattie, and the other is Maxine." Dedria said.

"Doc tells me you need to hear this next message. He says *there was nothing anyone could have done for him*," I said. "Your family immediately surrounded him. Even though he was at the training facility, he says he felt your arms around him when he left. He was not scared, and he did not feel any pain. Just a shift in pressure. Everything happened so fast."

Dedria was relieved Doc did not suffer. Thoughts of him struggling or in pain haunted her.

"He is shifting gears. Now, he wants me to talk about Florida," I said, "Does that make any sense?"

"Yes, we just got back from our family vacation. We have a condominium in Florida," Dedria said.

"Wow, it looks like he went with you. Doc also shows swinging doors and something with a leopard print on it," I said.

"We have swinging saloon doors in our home," Dedria said, "The leopard print is everywhere in our home. The bedding in Doc's crate has a leopard print cushion, and he loved his toy ducky. It has leopard spots on it. I also have a bathrobe with leopard print that I draped on the bed near his crate."

"No wonder I'm seeing it everywhere," I said, "Doc also says there are bells that ring. Do you understand this?"

"Absolutely!" Dedria said, "We hung bells on the doorknob so the dogs can ring them when they want to go outside. After Doc died, the bells would ring, but when I went to the door, he was asleep in the other room. That must have been Doc!"

As I closed the session down, one last message came through.

"Doc says the reason this happened is purposeful for your soul's growth," I said, "This experience has opened your heart and soul to new perspectives. He is proud of how much he helped you and will always be near to guide you. Like a guardian angel."

Dedria's grief shifted that day. The heaviness of guilt and remorse started to lift. Dedria realized that life continues after death, and Doc was alive and well in spirit. She felt like she could finally breathe again.

Several weeks later, the necropsy results confirmed what Doc already told us. The cause of death was the abnormal twisting of the intestines. Their veterinarian said some instances like this were fatal, and there was nothing anyone could have done to save him.

Doc's afterlife messages planted the seeds for healing and are Dedria's most treasured gifts.

As for those bells, they continue to ring even when no one is there.

Chapter 65

Cash

Frank could not bear to go outside anymore. It was just too hard to face his well-meaning neighbors when they asked him where Cash was. The tears welled in his eyes, and it was painful to tell the story again.

This loss cut him deeply as no one saw it coming. Not even me.

Cash was a nine-year-old American pit bull terrier mix who tipped the scales at about 130 pounds. I shared his incredible reincarnation story in my previous book.

During a communication session Frank had many years ago, his first dog, Captain, shared specific clues detailing his upcoming reincarnation.

One of the clues was the letter 'C.'

Frank wasn't entirely convinced the messages would add up to finding the reincarnated spirit of Captain again, but he set out with the highest intentions.

After an internet search, Frank was guided to an eight-week-old white American pit bull terrier with brown spots. Frank knew instantly that there was something special about this puppy.

Coincidentally, the clues Captain provided during his communication session fell into place except for the one about the letter C.

It wasn't until Frank got back home and took some pictures of his new pup that the last clue fell into place.

There was a mark on the pup's forehead in the shape of a C. No one had noticed it before, and the photos show an undeniable letter C. It was the last unmistakable clue from Captain, and Frank was surprised and overjoyed.

He named his new puppy Cash, who soon grew into a massive dog.

He was the equivalent of a brown and white tornado or a four-legged bulldozer.

The letter C had long since disappeared from his forehead, but Cash was the light of Frank's life.

The first sign of trouble started innocently enough as a trickle of blood from Cash's nose. Frank was concerned, so he looked closer but did not see anything. There were no wounds or blockages he could see.

Frank was relieved when the nosebleeds stopped. But a few weeks later, they started again. Frank took Cash into the veterinary clinic for a thorough exam. They couldn't find anything in his nasal cavity and prescribed some medication to stop the bleeding.

Cash was his usual exuberant self, yet Frank had a sense there was something more serious. One day, while they were playing in the yard, Cash's nose began to bleed and would not stop. Frank rushed Cash to the emergency clinic.

After a series of tests, the doctor called with the heartbreaking news. The X-rays revealed the source of the nosebleeds as a large cancerous tumor on Cash's spleen.

There was very little they could do about this aggressive type of cancer. The vet determined that the tumors had spread to other organs, and the prognosis was bleak.

The hopelessness and devastation hit Frank very hard.

He thought Cash would be coming home that day, but he had to make an impossible decision instead. He had to say goodbye to his beloved boy and best friend.

He would not risk the tumor rupturing or causing Cash pain. It was a horrible decision. While Cash was still under sedation, Frank let him go.

An overwhelming sense of heartache combined with deep sadness consumed him every day. So many thoughts ran through his mind.

He did his best to trust that Cash was with him and did not let doubts control his thoughts. He kept an open mind and, most importantly, watched for a sign that Cash was near.

Early one morning, just days after Cash transitioned, Frank was lying in bed. He heard a loud scratching sound coming from inside his bedroom wall.

Frank did not have any other pets. It wasn't a bird or a squirrel; it was too loud to be a small animal.

He inspected the area, trying to figure out the source of the scratching. He found nothing in or around the house.

Bewildered by this loud sound, it finally hit him. His heart skipped a beat when a wave of love washed over him. Frank knew from his past sessions with me that departed pets send scratching noises as a sign they are there.

Frank's heart began to melt as he realized his beloved Cash was letting him know he was with him. He was determined to watch for more signs.

A week later, Frank had to finish some chores and clean the rain gutters before the snow fell. He dreaded going in the backyard, which felt empty without Cash bouncing around. But it was early November, and the rain gutters needed to be cleaned.

While he was on the ladder, Frank noticed a tiny object moving around on the ledge. When he took a closer look, he saw something odd.

A ladybug was sitting on the rain gutter in plain sight, right where he had heard the scratching sounds just days earlier.

Most ladybugs were dormant in November, yet this one was alive and well. The recent cold temperatures confirmed what Frank already knew in his heart.

The ladybug was another sign from his boy, Cash.

Several weeks later, the next sign from Cash appeared. Frank went into the backyard and glanced over to Cash's favorite spot.

When he got closer, he noticed something on the grass. There was a pile of gray feathers. He thought that a bird had been attacked in his yard, but he didn't see any other indications that you would typically expect.

There was just a sizable pile of feathers in the grass. The feathers seemed to be placed there intentionally, and what struck him was odd as they were in the same spot where Cash used to lie in the sun.

Frank couldn't believe his eyes. He knew departed pets would send a feather, but this was a whole pile of feathers. He snapped a few photos to share with his wife Cheryl when she got home.

Feathers formed the letter 'C'

Later that afternoon, Frank told Cheryl about the strange feathers he found in the yard.

Excited and curious, they both went out to have a look. They could not believe what they saw. The pile of feathers had somehow been shaped into the letter C.

They had no idea how that happened. There was no wind that day, and no one else was in their backyard. They didn't have other pets or small children, and the yard was completely fenced in, so they ruled out everything except one conclusion.

It was another sign from Cash.

The signs continued when one afternoon Frank went out to the memorial area in his backyard for his three departed dogs, Captain, Doobie, and Cash.

As he approached the memorial, he saw something bright yellow beside the fence. He went over to inspect it. He could not believe his eyes. It was a brand-new plastic yellow butterfly with sparkles on the wings next to the dog's memorial.

Frank had never seen that butterfly before and had no clue why it would be there. Immediately, he knew it was another sign from Cash.

A yellow plastic butterfly appeared near the dog's memorial.

All the afterlife signs led to a huge surprise. Frank found a large feather at the foot of his bed. It was precisely where Cash used to sleep.

No one else was home, and no way for a feather to enter his room. There was no doubt in Frank's mind as to how that feather got there.

After Cash died, Frank hesitated to get another dog. Then one night, he had a vivid dream with numbers seven and eleven.

He understood them to be a possible date he would find his next pup. He also saw a dog's face with reddish-brown fur, with white on its nose. Although he didn't recognize the dog, Frank was excited that this could be his new pup.

Frank scheduled another session with me, hoping to gain more insight. He did not tell me about his dream or the coloring of the dog he saw

"I see a puppy with a reddish-brown face and a white smudge on his nose," I said, "There is also a row of dog kennels, but this is not a shelter. It looks like a private home."

Frank listened quietly.

"I also see the letter G," I said, "There is something significant about it, but I don't know what."

I asked Frank's departed dog, Doobie, if he could share anything about the new puppy.

"Doobie shows me the numbers seven and eleven, and he says the puppy will arrive soon. Does any of this make sense?" I asked.

Frank finally told me about his dream. Everything matched except the reference about the puppy arriving *soon*.

Takoda

Within a short time, Frank found a breeder with the type of puppy he was searching for.

He was guided to a row of dog kennels in the yard precisely as I had described them in our session.

Frank was shocked and amazed to see a pup with a reddish-brown face with a white smudge on the nose.

It was just like the pup in his dream and the pup I described. The clues were all falling into place again.

Just two more clues were left.

Frank got home and noticed the street address of the breeder started with the letter G on Gilia Drive.

Frank smiled as he looked at the calendar. It was the eleventh.

A sense of wonder washed over Frank. He quickly sent me the photos of his new pup and told me all about the clues. I still get goosebumps when I think about it.

Welcome home, Takoda. Welcome home.

Chapter 66

Reincarnation

Reincarnation is when a departed soul returns to Earth, merges into a new body, and lives a new life.

How they choose the new body or host varies with each soul.

The concept of reincarnation has fascinated humans for eons. Some cultures strongly believe in reincarnation, and others do not.

I was in the *not-sure category* when I began my animal communication journey. I was intrigued but not convinced that a soul reincarnates.

All that changed once the animals shared their reincarnation experiences.

Now, after more than two decades of connecting with departed pets and human spirits I believe all sentient beings can reincarnate if desired.

Many variables are involved, but reincarnation seems to be a combination of personal choice, soul progression, and of course, love.

While spiritual growth may be a large part of a soul's purpose to reincarnate, your companion may choose to come back to enhance your experience, their experience, or both of your experiences. Our companions are the icing on the cake of life and make everything richer.

Reincarnation is like graduating to the next level of enlightenment. The more times a soul reincarnates, the more knowledge and experience they gain, which carries forward to some degree to the next life.

The vibration of their frequency increases each time as well. Higher vibrational beings are joyful to be with and have an old soul feeling about them even at a young age.

Not every soul chooses to reincarnate.

Some souls prefer to stay in the glory of the afterlife and continue their journey in spirit form.

As you know, life on Earth is not easy. Being in the afterlife is very easy. You really cannot compare the two.

It is obvious why some prefer to stay in spirit form.

You will never miss your companion's reincarnation.

There are no set rules for reincarnation; everything can and will shift quickly, mainly because humans change their minds a lot. They change careers, move, and have families, which can alter reincarnation plans. If your companion decides to reincarnate and you move to a place that does not allow pets, they will patiently wait for another opportunity. You will never miss their reincarnation. They are destined to be with you.

Most animals reincarnate as animals, but some choose different hosts.

The most common reincarnation seems to be when the animal reincarnates as that same species of animal. Most dogs return as dogs, and most cats return as cats. But I have learned that exceptions can occur when animals reincarnate in human form and vice versa.

There are many different beliefs, too many to list here but some are based on karma and others based on traditions. There are unlimited ways a soul can return to physical form. This is the free-flowing adaptive nature of reincarnation at its best.

Reincarnation is not cloning.

It is a common misconception that your companion will be exactly as you remember them. That is not reincarnation. That is cloning. If your companion reincarnates, they will have a new body, personality, and life experience. You may see an essence of them the way they were before. That essence can vary from just a little to a lot.

They may display a familiar habit or sleep in the same spots. They may or may not maintain those traits because those things are not the purpose of reincarnation. You have been together many times and will come together many times in the future. Embrace the new version of your companion, no matter what level of essence you sense, and love them even more than you did the last time.

If your companion was a stray, had more than one caretaker, or a divorce split the family, they tend to gravitate to those with whom they had the strongest bond or the most profound connection. They may reincarnate to a past caretaker in a different lifetime or perhaps never. Again, many variables and circumstances can alter the outcome.

Lifespans can vary depending on how soon a soul returns.

When a companion animal chooses to return immediately, they tend to have a shorter-than-expected lifetime. The longer they spend in the glory of the afterlife, the longer their next lifetime seems to be.

There are always exceptions, and no two souls have the same experience, but the afterlife has restorative and rejuvenating benefits for souls who linger. Even though there is no linear time in the afterlife, there seems to be a direct connection between a longer life if that soul does not return immediately.

I wish I knew all the reasons why, but I believe the loving environment of the afterlife fuels the soul for eternity.

Begging, praying, or wishing cannot force a soul's return.

If it is not the highest and best for all involved for your companion to reincarnate, it will not happen. At least not for a very long time. That is probably not what you wanted to hear, but it is true. Some things are beyond your control, and the destiny of a soul is one of those things.

Invite them to come back again.

Remember, it is up to forces far more significant than you and me alone. Mysteries like this are intriguing; maybe you will have all the answers you seek one day. But for now, remember, ultimately, it is not up to you. You can invite your companion to return and if reincarnation is best for their soul they will return.

There are many different options when a soul decides to return.

It is a common belief that reincarnation can only happen with a newborn. That is just one of many misconceptions and myths.

Those who choose to return can do so in various ways. The four most common options are the *Newborn, Walk-in, Soul Sharing, and Drop-in* methods.

Newborn Method: This is when a companion animal leaves the body and spends a long time in the afterlife, commonly between three to five calendar years or longer. When a soul is ready for a new adventure, they wait for an opportunity to return. When everything is in alignment, they reincarnate. This occurs after conception or anytime during the birth process.

They may also merge into a newborn around the time the eyes open. Most newborns do not have distinctive personalities until their eyes open. A litter of puppies or kittens generally all act the same. It is around the time their eyes open, and the soul reincarnates, that a unique personality emerges.

Souls returning with this method tend to have an average lifespan.

Walk-in Method: This is when a companion dies and immediately returns to physical form by walking or merging into a new body. There is only a brief amount of time spent in the afterlife. The new body can be a newborn or even a few weeks old. Typically, the average lifespan of a Walk-in will be shorter than usual but intensely meaningful. There will be a lot of living in a short time. A soul may return to help you through a tough time even though they may not be here very long.

Soul Sharing: This method is when a companion returns and shares the body of an existing animal for the rest of the host animal's life. When permission is granted to share a body, lifetimes tend to be shorter than average because the body wears down faster with two souls. Specific behaviors will surface that remind you of your former companion mixed in with the behavior of your existing animal. It is almost like having two different companions rolled into one. Soul Sharing tends to be a slow realization that something unique happened as familiar behaviors emerge. Everyone benefits from the love that is shared in this method.

Drop-ins: With this method, a soul can drop in with the permission of the host animal and visit. These Drop-ins are an easy way for your departed companion to enjoy the physical connection with you again. They may visit once or twice, or they may visit often. There may be a specific toy they play with or unusual behavior that your existing companion never did before. These moments usually create a strong emotional response as your soul recognizes theirs. The lifespan of a Drop-ins tends to be average and the experience benefits both companions.

How do you know if a companion has reincarnated?

A skilled animal communicator or medium can determine if your beloved companion has reincarnated however, you know more than anyone. If you get a sense your companion has reincarnated, then chances are good they have. Your body and soul react when in the presence of a past life connection. It is an inner knowing, a gut feeling, or an indescribable connection between you. Trust your instincts above all else.

Billy

Billy was a white tabby cat with dark spots that Ann rescued as a tiny kitten. As he got older, Billy developed an unusual habit of climbing on the shelves in the pantry and ripping open bags of green split peas.

He did not eat the peas. He played with them. He chased them all over the floor. It was a crazy and unusual behavior that always brought a smile across Ann's face.

She let Billy have his fun despite the mess and diligently cleaned up the green mess when he lost interest.

When Billy transitioned many years later, Ann got a new kitten named Bella. She was gray with a patch of white on her nose. Ann felt an uncanny connection with her new kitty that she could not explain.

Bella seemed wiser than her young age and slept in the same spot that Billy did. When Ann gazed into Bella's eyes she felt she could see deep into her soul.

Early one morning, Ann heard strange noises from the kitchen.

She went to investigate and saw Bella chasing something on the floor. Split peas! Bella tore into a bag of split peas just like Billy used to. Green peas were everywhere, but Ann didn't care. She knew there was only one explanation in her mind. Her sweet Billy had dropped into Bella's body to say hello.

Only he could have influenced Bella to play with the split peas. It was a glorious moment that Ann cherished. Billy continued to pop in occasionally, and he always had a bag of split peas waiting for him in the pantry.

If you try hard enough, you can always find something good after a loss. While you may think that is impossible and there is nothing good about grief, this next chapter might change your mind.

Chapter 67

Raise Your Vibration For

More Signs

"Everything in life is vibration."~ Albert Einstein

A simple way to encourage signs from the afterlife is to raise your vibration. Every living organism, every inanimate object, every thought, feeling, and desire has a unique vibration, just like a fingerprint.

Science has proven that solid material has a lower frequency than liquids.

Even colors have a vibration. Red has the lowest frequency on the color spectrum, and violet has the highest.

Emotions such as love, joy, and gratitude vibrate at a higher frequency than grief, despair, and sorrow.

When you are happy, you feel elated because your vibration is high.

Likewise, you feel so down when grieving because your vibration is low.

This is the law of vibration and the more closely you pay attention to it the more likely you are to sense energetic messages and signs from your companion.

We are vibrational beings, so we can intuitively sense the good or bad vibes of people and situations.

That creepy feeling you get from someone is the law of vibration in action.

Companion animals are good at feeling the vibes of strangers.

Their reactions tell the story of whether you should trust that person or situation.

You can tap into that frequency when you allow your intuition to guide you. Your body will react to these unseen forces.

When you get goosebumps, chills, or feel nauseous your senses are picking up on the vibrational energy around you.

There are many ways to raise your vibration

The simplest way to raise your vibration is to do small things that make you feel better.

That may be a challenge when you are in pain and grieving, but every effort you make is one step closer, as your actions are cumulative.

Crystals

One of the most natural ways to raise your vibration is with crystals. Crystals are your best friend on your journey into healing. The Earth, sun, moon, and stars powerfully charge them.

Their energy connects with your intention. Crystals amplify your thoughts just by having them near you. When you wear them and hold them their power is even greater.

Your thoughts go out into the Universe, amplified by the crystals, and create your future.

Hold positive, loving thoughts when working with crystals.

Your thoughts give your crystals a task to complete and can provide powerful results.

How Crystals Work

Each crystal carries a unique vibration. These vibrations realign or recalibrate your energy with theirs to raise your vibration and reach a higher state of being. This feels like an uplifting boost of positive energy, like a midday caffeine boost.

The crystal amplifies your intention by holding strong and positive energy, so you manifest faster.

When you are in tune with the higher frequency of the crystal, it is much easier to move past emotional, physical, or spiritual blockages.

Visit a local crystal store and see which crystals feel good in your hand or call to you.

Simple Ways to Raise Your Vibration:

1. Take a walk or go for a hike.

2. Get a small fountain and listen to the water bubbling.

3. Get creative – Draw, paint, or write in your journal.

4. Write a letter to your companion.

5. Create a memorial to honor your companion.

6. Watch a feel-good movie with a friend.

7. Grab a cup of tea or coffee at your favorite place in town.

8. Listen to your favorite music.

9. Volunteer – Acts of kindness expand the heart immediately.

What matters is that you do one small thing at least once a day, preferably more, to raise your vibration.

Chapter 68

Hold My House

If I asked you to put your hand out, palm facing upward, and choose from either holding my hat or my house, which would you choose?

My house would be too heavy, and my hat is lightweight and made from fabric.

You would probably choose my hat.

Now, let's say I asked you to keep holding my hat outward in the palm of your hand for the next few hours. After a while, the hat that was so light will begin to feel heavy.

Finally, I ask you to hold that hat for days, weeks, months, or years. It would not take long for that hat to feel as heavy as my house.

The longer you hold my hat, the heavier it gets.

Your arm starts to ache, you get uncomfortable, and you cannot focus on anything except the pain my hat is causing you.

I will try to tell you that it is not the hat causing all the pain.

It is holding onto it that hurts so much.

Grief is precisely the same.

It is not grief causing the pain.

It is your choice to hold on to it.

Holding onto grief causes even more discomfort and makes it hard to focus on anything except the source of your pain.

Grief is complicated and has many layers, but this example is easy to remember.

The longer you hold onto grief, the heavier it weighs upon you.

You can hold onto the grief for as long as you want.

There is no set time, nor is there a wrong or right way. It just depends on your ability to manage all that pain.

If it were me, I would let go of the hat before it became too heavy of a burden. But that is just me.

You oversee that decision, and I will honor whatever you decide.

Take small steps if you are not ready to release the hat. Just put it down for short periods. Allow yourself to take a break. Walk away unburdened and free to move around without pain.

It is okay, and you have permission to feel better. Then keep adding more baby steps. Set the hat down for more extended periods.

You will find life is better in many ways after you put the hat down.

You do not have to feel bad about putting the hat down. The hat is perfectly fine when it is not in your hand.

The hat can still exist without you.

You can go back and look at the hat occasionally, and you may even miss parts of the hat, but I will bet you will not miss all that pain and discomfort.

Remember this, put the hat down before it becomes a house.

While my analogies are a bit crazy, you may find they do make sense.

The tight grip that grief holds will begin to loosen.

It will not happen overnight, but you will begin to see things in a new light in time.

That means you have a brand-new chance to start your healing journey.

You can start over as many times as you need to.

I will not judge you.

You may want to flip-flop back and forth as you think about your time together and perhaps the things you would do differently.

It's okay to do that, but I hope you let go of any thoughts or memories that no longer serve you.

If something makes you sad, let it go.

If it makes you feel bad, let it go.

It is up to you to release those thoughts.

The road to healing is sometimes a bumpy ride. Many potholes, speed bumps, and detours lie ahead, but a peaceful destination lies ahead.

You have already endured the worst part of your story, and now it is time for you to relax, breathe, and allow your heart to expand.

Just let the cruise control take over.

You have earned this time to rest, fuel up, and restore your soul.

I think your beloved companions would want that more than anything else, don't you?

Chapter 69

Legacy

A unique way to honor that pet you can't forget is to live their legacy.

What are their gifts, guidance, or teachings that you can carry into the world?

Honor their life by living yours through how they enriched yours.

For instance, if your companion gave you unconditional love, live the rest of your life by providing unconditional love.

If they were your best friend, then be a best friend.

If they provided companionship, give a needy animal companionship.

When you live your life honoring them, their legacy lives on.

Chapter 70

From the Author

"Goodbyes are only for those who love with their eyes.

Because for those who love with heart and soul,

there is no such thing as separation."

~ Rumi

This is the section where I am supposed to list all my accomplishments and credentials, but I would rather talk about you.

You are the most important part of this book.

I was guided to share my experiences with you from countless afterlife sessions to be a beacon of light on your healing journey.

Even though I will never be able to feel how much pain you are in or the depth of your grief, I am very familiar with saying goodbye to someone I love.

I have had a lot of practice.

More than two years have passed since I started this book.

During that time, I lost eight of my beloved companions.

Each loss set me back further than the previous one. When I felt like I could finally focus on writing again, I would lose another.

I am a private griever, so I disappeared from the radar. Much like the animals, I am a master at hiding my pain.

Maybe you are like me. Getting older, loss and grief takes on a whole new perspective.

The losses seem to hit us harder, and we feel them more deeply.

Perhaps our own mortality makes us more aware that we are moving closer to our own transition date.

That alone should motivate you to grasp every day with utter gratitude and appreciation with desperate abandon.

We may have suffered a terrible loss, but we loved too.

We gave love, and we received love, didn't we?

You deserve a joyful life. Create that life starting today.

The only one holding you back is you.

I can guide you, but you must take inspired action.

Be passionate about your healing journey. Commit to healing with as much integrity as you committed to loving the companion you just lost.

Nothing can stop you with that level of determination.

We have covered a lot of ground since that first chapter, and I hope you have found a few golden nuggets of wisdom within these pages to help you move forward.

I have laid the groundwork and provided many tools and insights so you can take the next step.

I know you can do it.

It may seem like the dark clouds never leave or the emptiness will never fade, but a shift will begin once you commit to moving forward.

Knowing that your beloved companions will always be near, and you will see them again someday is a comfort we all desire.

This is your time to shine.

Surround yourself with others who align with your new perspective and goals. Remove yourself from those who do not support you.

Those with the least knowledge about a topic tend to have the strongest opinion against it.

Ignore them.

If you have a dream, go for it.

Don't just think about it.

Don't just talk about it.

Do your dream.

It is never too late, and it will make all the difference in the world.

If you are considering a new companion, there are so many need a forever home.

As a kid, I dreamed of opening an animal sanctuary, so I set sail and made it happen.

In 2021, I launched my non-profit, **Painted Rain Ranch Animal Sanctuary**, a 501(c)(3) charitable organization. We provide a forever home to elderly, special needs, injured, and abandoned companion animals.

We rescue the pets that no one else wants.

They are often overlooked at shelters. Their medical issues or behavior problems prevent would-be adopters from giving them a chance.

At Painted Rain Ranch Animal Sanctuary, we believe no companion animal should die alone or in a facility.

They deserve love and a final refuge too. Our resident animals enjoy our 30-acre ranch in Eastern Washington until their last breath.

The proceeds from my books and courses benefit these deserving souls.

I created the life I always dreamed of, and guess what?

If I can do it, so can you.

There is nothing special about me.

In fact, I am incredibly dull and ordinary.

My days are filled with scooping poop, cleaning up unmentionables, medicating, and feeding the animals.

Massive amounts of love are abundantly given and received on the ranch.

If you can adopt a deserving companion, please do. One simple act of kindness can help so much. If you cannot adopt, please consider donating to non-profits like mine so those who dedicate their lives to rescuing animals can continue to save lives.

Find us here:

www.PaintedRainRanch.org

We are family-operated, all-volunteer and rely on donations to save lives and care for our residents.

What you can do for me

If this book helped you in any way, please consider donating to Painted Rain Ranch Animal Sanctuary. Every dollar makes a difference.

I would love to hear from you!

Send an email! Just visit my website and click Contact Karen. I welcome your feedback and will never get tired of hearing that my books helped you or that special pet you can't forget.

Post a review

If you feel so inclined, please post a review on AMAZON or AUDIBLE or wherever you can.

Share this book on social media

The greatest compliment I can receive is when you tell others about my book.

Share with a friend

Please share this book with a friend in need or gift them a copy.

Order more books

I would be thrilled if you ordered a bunch of copies from me, so be sure to contact my office for bulk discounts.

Download my free mobile app

On your device search the App Store or Google Play for **Pet Loss Hope & Healing**. For the best experience ALLOW notifications and sign-up as a MEMBER for Member's Only content, animal communication training, and much more.

I have no doubt you were guided my way, so thank you for trusting me and reading all the way to the end.

In time, you may want to go back and revisit some of the stories I shared. As you move forward, your mind can absorb more information, and more golden nuggets of wisdom will be revealed.

There will be days ahead when you are a warrior and others where you are broken. Most days are a bit of both — some days, you may hold onto the pain because it feels like your last link to your angel. I promise you it is not.

Keep showing up. Keep trying and keep fighting.

I do not believe that traumatic events make us stronger. Overcoming those tragedies and pulling through the darkness makes us stronger.

I doubt many others will understand how much strength it takes to pull yourself out of a dark place. I am so proud of you if you have done that today or any day.

It is always okay to ask for help if your burden is too heavy.

Find a professional to guide you.

There is a well-deserved and meaningful future that awaits you. And don't worry; there will always be that one special companion, the one that changed you forever, who will always be near. You may have loved many, but one holds the key to your heart and soul, and you will be reunited one day.

Your beloved companion is not the darkness you endured. They are the light within that refuses to surrender when you realize not that they died, but they lived, and their life gave you so many beautiful memories.

Make your companions life more important than their death.

My greatest wish is for you to find the courage to pursue your goals regardless of the opinions of others. Their comments can hurt, especially regarding the afterlife or animal communication.

I know because I have heard it all. In the last twenty-six years, I have been called every rude name in the book and none of it matters. Perhaps my career in law enforcement gave me thick skin.

Instead, I focus on those who are enlightened, open-minded, and willing to discover new skills and perspectives.

I found my path, and so can you.

You are beautiful and capable of anything you set your mind to.

May you find your strength today and take inspired action.

With love and heartfelt gratitude,

Karen A. Anderson

www.KarenAnderson.net

"Let go of what no longer serves you.

Peace lies just below the surface.

There is no finding it, only committing to it.

It is there, waiting for you to make room in your heart.

Hold on tightly to the love and legacy

from your special companion.

The pet you can't forget.

For they were the best thing that ever happened to you.

And you were the best thing that ever happened to them."

~ Karen A. Anderson

Chapter 71

About Karen

Karen A. Anderson is an esteemed author known for her heartwarming and insightful books that explore the afterlife of animals and the profound connections we share with our beloved pets.

Karen's ability to understand animals began as a child and later resurfaced when she was a deputy sheriff in Colorado. When animals on crime scenes began to share accurate details about her cases, Karen embraced this unique opportunity to develop her intuitive skills and began a robust twenty-six-year career as an award-winning animal communicator.

With two best-selling books already captivating readers, including "The Amazing Afterlife of Animals: Messages and Signs From Our Pets on the Other Side" and "Hear All Creatures: The Journey of an Animal Communicator," Karen documents her fascinating experiences from deputy to pet psychic with actual stories.

Karen's writing not only touches readers' hearts but also offers a sense of hope and healing. Her heartwarming stories, infused with actual messages from the afterlife, bring solace to those who have experienced the loss of a cherished animal companion.

In addition to her writing, Karen offers courses and coaching for individuals seeking to enhance their own animal communication abilities.

Her dedication to spreading love and understanding between humans and animals extends to her non-profit organization, Painted Rain Ranch Animal Sanctuary, a 501(c)(3) non-profit organization, that provides a final refuge for unwanted and special needs companion animals.